The End of Divine Truthiness:
Love, Power, and God

The End of Divine Truthiness: Love, Power, and God

Powerful Buddhist-Christian-Taoist Love

PAUL JOSEPH GREENE

Foreword by Paul R. Sponheim

WIPF & STOCK · Eugene, Oregon

THE END OF DIVINE TRUTHINESS: LOVE, POWER, AND GOD
Powerful Buddhist-Christian-Taoist Love

Wipf & Stock
An Imprint of Wipf and Stock Publishers
199 W. 8th Ave., Suite 3
Eugene, OR 97401

www.wipfandstock.com

PAPERBACK ISBN: 978-1-4982-8031-0
HARDCOVER ISBN: 978-1-4982-8033-4
EBOOK ISBN: 978-1-4982-8032-7

Manufactured in the U.S.A.   JULY 21, 2017

*For all who have been harmed by
bullies and tyrants of every sort.
Powerful Love is on your side.*

We are caught in an inescapable network of mutuality, tied in a single garment of destiny. Whatever affects one directly, affects all indirectly.

MARTIN LUTHER KING, JR.,
"LETTER FROM A BIRMINGHAM JAIL"

Contents

CONTENTS

Foreword

An increasing number of thinking people are asking whether religion is a good thing—and many of them are leaving the churches, mosques, and synagogues. On the one hand the daily news brings unfailingly new word of violence perpetrated in the name of religion. In this bold and creative book, Paul Joseph Greene offers a deep and sweeping analysis of the disease afflicting religion and the resultant disaffection and departure. He's operating at a sick bed here and is appropriately thorough in his diagnosis and ambitious in his prognosis. Some of the disturbed and dispirited may not be able to swallow all the medicine made available, but they will be stimulated toward some kind of health-enhancing change by this doctor's work.

His ally in diagnosis is Stephen Colbert, whose biting derision has been viewed by millions in the long-running *The Colbert Report* and the more recent *The Late Show with Stephen Colbert*. A little humor does help when you approach a sacred cow. Whence comes all this religiously driven violence? The buck stops where it must, in the image of God and our knowledge of God. After all, if you represent a God who is all-wise, all-knowing, and all-powerful, there's no wonder that you might find differences of opinion offensive, even dangerous.

The sense that the practice of religion is morally offensive readily coexists with a quieter sense that the conceptual edifice constructed on faith's grounds is in a state of collapse. Again the difficulty goes to the front of the line: the concept of the divine. The problem seems to be that our experience of real life is contradicted by how we are told to understand the alleged Creator of that life. Life is experienced as a flowing thing, where borders are permeable and our relationships contribute materially to the identity we claim for ourselves. But God, we are told, is unchanging and "wholly other" than the life of give and take that we know in the tears and laughter of our days. There is coherence-straining talk in religion about God taking on suffering somehow—often violently at that—but the underlying concept of

God reigns through it all. It stretches our resources for belief to the break-ing point. It seems better to travel light.

Greene's critique is devastating in exposing the moral and conceptual offense evoked by "divine truthiness," drawing on Colbert's term. But hap-pily this book proposes an alternative that is desperately needed. Instead of "giving back the entrance ticket" (Dostoevsky) he expands the venue for the encounter with religion and religious difference. He draws deeply on three distinctly different religious traditions: Buddhism, Christianity, and Taoism. Moreover, as he engages these faiths he does not back away from the cognitive challenge entailed in the encounter. At the center of the book is the recogni-tion that "it matters what we say about God and humanity," for good or for ill.

Greene's analysis calls us to a work of excavation, digging down deeply in a description of the actual experience of human beings beneath the battle of beliefs. He identifies mutual becoming as the pulse of the experiencing that comes together in the flow of our daily lives. This is not an appeal to some kind of featureless unity. He probes the meaning of empathy and offers an illuminating set of polarities: solitude and solidarity in mutual-ity and gratitude, and generosity in reciprocity. There's a given-ness in this description and there's a call as well. It rings right.

Thus he proceeds to counter our love affair with "controlling power" and opens us to recognizing the genuine power in persuasion. One senses Mahatma Gandhi and Martin Luther King Jr. cheering him on in his evo-cation of an understanding of power in transformation toward the full flourishing of all creatures, human and not human. Power and love have often been juxtaposed in the turbulent tale of religion. Greene sees them coming together in an availing power that reverses the learned oppositions that have normed our beliefs and behaviors. His excavation has facilitated the reclaiming of genuinely progressive and nonviolent resources in the religious traditions he studies.

A close look at many traditional doctrines of the divine may bring the seeker to ask whether the divine omnis must stand or fall together. With an appeal to a powerful "Omnicaritas," Greene makes clear that they do not. Here is hope for fruitful interreligious conversation and conceptual clarity in the truth claims to be made about God *and* the world.

Paul R. Sponheim
Professor Emeritus of Systematic Theology
Luther Seminary
St. Paul, Minnesota

Some Acknowledgments

This book is a collaboration of countless generous and loving people. In fact, it would be impossible to exhaustively catalogue the many contributions from so many people.

So, let me try, anyway. I wish to express my gratitude to people I have never met, including the many authors and theologians I quote, and the comedian and cultural commentator Stephen Colbert. His wit, honesty, and genius give me hope for humanity. But, in the very next breath, I also need to thank the people who strain my ability to hope: in a funny way, the really terrible people who make news all the time—all the time!—are the ones who have galvanized my vision. They have helped me see real problems with things as they are, and have pushed me to find an alternative.

Mostly, though, I am constantly inspired and amazed and humbled by the bright, thoughtful hearts of people I *do* know. For instance, my students keep me going. They wear me out and never stop teaching me. Among my hundreds of remarkable students I can name only a few whose generosity humbles me and makes me long to be better at what I do: Ari Peterson, Lisa Clark, Reies Romero, Amy Amsler, Nimo Mohamed, and Anna Shilongo. Come to think of it, a decade or so of adjunct teaching on four campuses is nothing if not a long education in reality. And, to be clear, I am *think*ing those years of enriching experience in spite of the financial impoverishment.

Family contributes in ways that elude expression. Thanks to John and Betty Greene, Pat and Larry Enwall, Mike Greene and Wes Gadsden, Chris Greene and Erin Hoffman (Erin, for always asking when this book would be published), and Jack and Luella Greene. Thank you to my brilliant, creative, and generous sister, CarrieAnn Jones, and your house full of unbearably lovable guys: Ashby, Ki Bae, and Ryu Utting. Thanks to my mountain man brother, Dan Thoemke, for recognizing a special sort of loving relational power in me, even way back when we were kids—and thanks Kelly Charbonneau for taking excellent care of Dan. And thanks to my loving mom, Jan Eigenbrodt, for believing in me even when second grade, third grade, *and* fourth grade were terrible. Somehow you knew I could get better, and you've never stopped cheerleading me.

Thanks to Chris Stedman, the witty and candid author of *Faitheist*, for helping me to see myself as a public theologian. Fond memorial thanks go to Russ Connors, Br. Michael Collins, and the Rev. Cody Unterseher, whose encouragement of my potential cannot be overestimated. Warm thanks to my teachers and professors through the years: Bill Cahoy, Charles Bobertz, Columba Stewart, JP Earls, Bernard Evans, Ron Svitak, Guillermo Hansen, and Paul Chung. Thanks to Trish Sullivan Vanni for asking me why I wasn't teaching college as an adjunct, and showing me how to get started. The Ven. David Selzer, Executive Archdeacon of the Anglican Church of Canada, Diocese of Ottawa—thank you for your advocacy and friendship across more than 20 years. Gratitude to my friend and colleague Paul Francis Miller for teaching me on a regular basis the meaning of perseverance and wholesome integrity of life. Affectionate thanks to the tender and generous geniuses of the Theologians of the Round Table—Kiara Jorgenson, Alex Blondeau, Derek Kent Maris, Dana Scopatz, Josh de Keijzer, Tom Watson, and David Smoker—lovingly hosted in the home of our brilliant professor and advisor, Lois Malcolm. Huge thanks to Process and Faith friends and collaborators: Kirsten Mebust, Lynn Lorenzen, Jeanyne Slettom, Jonathan Davis, David Grant Smith, and Charles Yancey. And a special word of thanks goes to my colleagues at St. Catherine University—Vince Skemp, Bill McDonough, Rhodora Beaton, Christine Luna Munger, Colleen Carpenter, Elaine James, Claire Bischoff, Anh-Hoa Thi Nguyen, Gloria Blaha, Cyndy Krey, and Jeff Weiberg—for your generosity and hospitality in helping me take my place alongside you in my professional home.

In twelfth grade (a very long time ago) I wrote a novel for a creative writing course. My English teacher, Sue Wiborg, was wonderful. She taught me the meaning of good humor and tolerance by accepting my daily submission of twenty to thirty pages, even though my project was far in excess of the requirements of the course. Thank you for encouraging my writing.

As for this exact book . . . Thanks to all the bright, generous, thoughtful folks at Wipf & Stock: Nathan Rhoads, Matthew Wimer, Jana Wipf, and Brian Palmer.

My excellent friend Mike Hitzelberger and my excellent professor and mentor Paul R. Sponheim (author of many great books, including *Love's Availing Power*) each unflinchingly read the first draft of this book—*all 537 pages of the behemoth I handed them*. And they commented on the whole thing. And they even talked to me after they finished. They even still seem to like me. Here's a little proof: Professor Sponheim wrote the foreword. You can thank them for their input, making this a much more humane endeavor. And I hope you'll also join me in thanking Megan Hazen: when she saw what I handed her, she simply did not read it—it was too much. She was right. Her wisdom spoke volumes. And she still likes me too—but probably because she opted out of the 537-page version.

Further along the way, my friends Joan Wingert and Jill Zasadny offered to give my book a read-through. At first I was grateful, expecting some gentle and good-natured encouragement—but then I was wholeheartedly overwhelmed: they commented on every paragraph, asked demanding questions, suggested refinements, challenged and pushed me to find the heart I'd been journeying toward. If there is a page that makes sense to you, join me in thanking Joan and Jill for helping to polish this book to its final form.

Before I finish up . . . All this thanking is one thing. But, the book that follows is no doubt flawed because I am flawed, incomplete because I am incomplete, insufficient because I am insufficient. The thanks go out to all the people who have helped to *start* this conversation. Just because we cannot speak the final and perfect word, doesn't mean we must keep silent.

Finally . . . Not a word of this book, nor the gladness in my life, would be possible without the most generous, hard-working, patient, kind, tender, creative, ingenious, goading, loving, and outrageously smart person in my life: Tim Greene. If anyone has heard an idea from me in its most flagrantly unprepared state, it would have to be Tim. His support is astonishing. His patient endurance is miraculous.

Thanks and love to all of you, and apologies for those whose names I have omitted:

I am because we are.

(Please Don't Skip the) Introduction

The rise of authoritarian rulers is nothing new. And the inclination of some people to follow such dictators is also nothing new. So, on the one hand, we shouldn't be surprised when despots assume power over a society. On the other hand, our cynicism shouldn't be so complete that we are paralyzed into thinking there's nothing we can do about it. The real scandal is not the arrival of tyranny. The real scandal is the failure to respond to tyranny, to reverse it, and to restore the trajectory of justice. Tyranny has a long history, not just in politics, but also in religion. And it's time to *do something* about the scandalous failure to reply.

This book scrutinizes some of the theological roots that empower tyrannical attitudes that enforce structures of oppression on vulnerable people. It is about the theological underpinnings that turn everyday people into tiny tyrants who imitate big tyrants—even tyrants as big as the supposedly divine one, called God. Every time someone uses their strength to harmfully overpower someone else, we are all dehumanized. Every time someone beats up their kid, or batters their partner, human potential is diminished. Every time someone demeans another by mockery or name-calling, human dignity dwindles. As the beloved actor Meryl Streep said in a short speech in 2017, humiliation functions by a trickle-down effect:

> this instinct to humiliate, when it's modeled . . . by someone powerful, it filters down into everybody's life, because it kind of gives permission for other people to do the same thing. Disrespect invites disrespect. Violence incites violence. When the powerful use their position to bully others, we all lose.[1]

1. Friedman, "Here's the Full Transcript."

Streep is right. In fact, perhaps the deepest indignity comes when we define God as the Supreme Tyrant, the Ultimate Bully of the Universe, and then little human tyrannical bullies use that definition as the foundation for humiliations, oppressions, devastations, impoverishments, and degradations of every sort. The divine humiliator trickles down to human humiliators, and causes untold sufferings.

In light of religiously rooted immiserations, the outspoken intellectual, accomplished author, and skilled debater Dr. Sam Harris unleashes rationality against the many terrors motivated by religious faiths: "At the heart of every totalitarian enterprise one sees outlandish dogmas, poorly arranged, but working ineluctably like gears in some ludicrous instrument of death."[2] He minces no words, because the stakes are too high. Religions and faiths formed in the image of totalitarian killers have heaped up a history, the "catalog of horrors [from which] could be elaborated upon indefinitely."[3] He does not exaggerate.

We are long overdue to exercise extreme honesty about the terrors that have flowed out of incoherent theologies that make a mockery out of religious claims about love. Now, that kind of honesty will mean genuinely purging the obviously dangerous theologies from our minds and hearts. Honesty will require a new commitment to a wholesome path. The violent exercise of supposedly divine power has translated into the exercise of violent human power for too many centuries. We are at a crossroads: either the atheists are right, and it is time to ask God to retire, or there is a path forward with the God who is actually love—the God who empowers loving human action.

I lean toward the latter because the simple fact that the vast majority of people alive today are devoted to religious ways, devoted to God—to the point that they would never consider dispensing with their faith. That presents an immense potential for a reformed understanding of God. The hope and promise inside every page of *The End of Divine Truthiness* is that there is in fact a robust and reliable alternative wisdom about love-filled power, variously expressed in Buddhism, Christianity, and Taoism, so that the religions do not need to be abandoned. If we are guided and inspired by their best, the religions can be a force for innovative revolution. They can harness the vitality of faith and religion for the purpose of ennobling the world. In these pages I look back to a few religious wisdoms not in some

2. Harris, *End of Faith*, 101.
3. Ibid., 106.

nostalgic effort to preserve the past. No. This is an effort to investigate some religious truths for their revolutionary trajectories, in the hope that we may translate that insurgent power into a trajectory of progress calibrated for our day. A vision like that is a bountiful hope for a better future.

Yes: it is important to judge movements, religions, and ideologies based on the actual outcomes of their implementation. Being honest about terrifying horrors can help remove their power to proliferate. That kind of clear-eyed judgment can be the source of urgency for change. It gives us the capacity to exile the dangerous elements of religion and faith. One approach would be to conclude that there is nothing worthwhile or redeemable in religions with violent histories, so they must be utterly removed. But another, more refined approach is also possible. We can fearlessly name the wrong and dangerous elements, and banish precisely those. Then out of that wreckage, we can resurrect the wholesome elements that transform faith into energy to empower the world toward vast, powerful, authentic love.

That means power does not have to be necessarily bad in itself. Power is a symbol for the energy by which influence is exerted, and is made manifest. In this book we are on the lookout for wrongly calibrated, or dangerously applied power. To help hone our sensitivity toward alarming abuses of power, we shall call on the satirical genius of Stephen Colbert—specifically, his word *truthiness*—to give us a category for naming the dehumanizing elements in religion. Any theology with wicked powers that ruin love is a *divine truthiness* that requires eradication. We have been intoxicated with the wrong sort of power for too long. It's time to sober up, so we have better prospects for a better future.

The key to developing a brighter future is enacting power and love that do not exterminate one another. In 1967 the Rev. Dr. Martin Luther King, Jr. spoke on August 16 in Atlanta, Georgia, precisely on the issue of love and power. He taught the audience that "one of the great problems of history is that the concepts of love and power have usually been contrasted as opposites, polar opposites, so that love is identified with a resignation of power, and power with a denial of love."[4] The simple, ordinary (or as we shall see, "truthy") wisdom of the world pits love against power, and power against love. King demands that we engage our whole selves in a total effort to banish that absurd dichotomy. No mindless or half-hearted effort will do. Rather, "what is needed is a realization that power without

4. King, "Where Do We Go from Here?"

love is reckless and abusive, and that love without power is sentimental and anemic."[5] King sees the truth because he thoroughly understands that the power consistent with love is undeniably non-violent. The truth is, love and power require one another. They make one another to fully exist. And when either is deprived of the other, both are ruined.

Whereas King employs a Christian theology only, I hope the addition of an informal interreligious conversation with Buddhism and Taoism here will fortify the truth of powerful love to make it accessible to a wider audience for our day. So, in the undying hope to abandon deadly ideologies of terrifying power, and in that spirit to rally the faithful of the world to the side of genuine, powerful love, I call not for the end of faith[6], but rather for *the end of divine truthiness*. And that means a new beginning for powerful love.

---

5. Ibid.

6. This book is *definitely not* a "response" to or critique of Sam Harris's book, *The End of Faith*. In fact, I did not know of Harris's book until *after* I wrote and titled the first draft of this book—and a smart friend alerted me to the parallel titles. This book is, rather, a *different* response to terrifying elements of religion and theology. I have no doubt that, when they are faced with the difficult truths about religion and theology, many people *will* need to take the atheist path. But, this book is for those who wish to retain religious notions like God and divinity in the work toward a better future. This book's appeal to three world religions endeavors to chart a non-contentious, interreligious way forward that emphasizes the wholesome, helpful, and loving aspects of religions by expelling the dangerous elements. The titular parallelism reflects the fact that we both recognize that something has to end in order for a new way to arise.

Part 1

Truthiness

Truthiness comes from the gut, because brains are overrated.[1]
STEPHEN T. COLBERT, DFA

1. Colbert, *The Late Show*, season 1, episode 178.

Chapter 1

A Tornadic and Murderous God?

What do we mean by *God*? What do we mean when we say the word *God*? Lots of people use the word *God*, but it's doubtful they really mean the same thing by it. Does God hear prayers? Does God answer prayers? Does God reward? Does God punish? Does God care? Does God suffer? Does God enforce the divine will on creatures? Is God merciful? Is God a king or emperor? Is God a provider? Is God male? Is God violent? Is God a wrathful tyrant? Is God magnanimous? Is God an owner? Is God omnipotent? Is God petty? Is God an absolute moralist? Is God just? Is God statically perfect? Is God jealous? Is God a distant, uninvolved creator who set everything in motion and forgot about it? Is God a supernatural invader, picking winners and losers in everyday affairs? Is God one? Is God Trinity? Is God angry? Is God slow to anger? Is God gentle? Is God love? These sorts of questions (*and so many more!*) are obscured whenever we assume everyone means the same thing when they use the word *God*. The truth is, there isn't one solitary definition of God. Symbols, words, philosophies, categories, religions, and ideas of God try to answer those questions. As we shall see, some of those symbols of God raise serious questions that demand an answer. To begin our exploration, let's focus on a couple of common illustrations that might inspire us to be really clear about who we think God is, and what we think God might actually be like.

The Tornadic God

On Monday, May 20, 2013, an EF5 tornado with a width of at least 1.3 miles, and wind speeds over 200 miles per hour, leveled Moore, Oklahoma, including two elementary schools. On MSNBC, I heard a woman describe how her father, "By the grace of God . . . just went into the closet, the only room standing." As she spoke, she pointed to the pile of rubble behind her,

3

with the closet door standing intact.[1] If I heard her right, God's grace is stingily measured out in the barest minimum to stop just the tiniest amount of damage. That can't be right.

In a blog post about that same horrifying tornado, Carol Megathlin wrote the following: "We didn't have to ask the people of Oklahoma where God was. A man named James Moody stood before the ruins of his house and dialed Fox News. As anchor Shepard Smith asked about the devastation surrounding him, Moody said, 'I am a believer in Jesus, and by the grace of God, me and my children are alive. And our house is . . . we can repair it. But what is really valuable is relationships.'"[2] Of *course*, human relationships are more valuable than possessions. That is a wholesome truth. Unlike people, possessions can be replaced and repaired. But do we really mean to say that the God who destroyed more than 2,400 homes in Moore, Oklahoma, was waiting to hear your prayer and supplication not to kill you and your family? When we meet *people* who act like that, we call them murderers and monsters. So, why isn't a *God* who behaves like that a monster?

We have a right and a responsibility to question the so-called grace of a God who abuses with such devastating violence. In her blog, Megathlin goes on to say that "a woman named Micah called Fox [News and said] this: 'We know God's in control. We're believers. We prayed that God would save our house but we also prayed that if God didn't, He would get us through. And He will. And we're gonna be OK.'"[3]

This God who is in utter control is the saver, the comforter, the rebuilder, and the victimizer all rolled into one. It sounds more like the abuser in a violent relationship than the loving God of the universe. But these examples from this particular tornado are just the beginning. The coverage of any natural disaster is littered with similar remarks. Do we actually love and worship the Abuser God, the Tornadic God, who rewards the faithful by ruining their possessions but saving their lives, while punishing the supposedly faithless by killing them? Something is amiss.

The Murderous God of an Elementary School Shooting

On Friday, December 14, 2012, in Newtown, Connecticut, a man used a gun, bullets, and the energy of his life to take the lives of twenty Sandy

1 Matthews, *Hardball with Chris Matthews.*

2. Megathlin, "God of the Tornado."

3. Ibid.

Hook Elementary school children, six school staff, his own mother, and finally himself. No one knows what to say in moments like this. But in these moments we mumble, utter, and declare so many things about God. Do we really mean these things? Or are we making excuses for God? It was disheartening to hear how many people, President Obama included, said that God *called those children to heaven*. Actually, in his difficult effort to comfort, the President quoted Jesus, and went on from there:

> "Let the little children come to me," Jesus said, "and do not hinder them, for to such belongs the kingdom of heaven." Charlotte, Daniel, Olivia, Josephine, Ana, Dylan, Madeline, Catherine, Chase, Jesse, James, Grace, Emilie, Jack, Noah, Caroline, Jessica, Benjamin, Avielle, Allison, God has called them all home.[4]

At first hearing, maybe we don't recognize any trouble because this is such a common theology. But, *God called them all home*? Really? Does it feel loving and comforting to say something like that? Do we actually think this is a loving God "calling" his children back to him? What can that possibly mean? Are we saying it is God's loving plan to have people murdered as the means by which they are called back to God? Sounds extremely disturbing to me. I am not leveling a charge specifically against the President. He is merely expressing an altogether ordinary confusion about God. Hovering above all statements of this kind is the haunting specter of a God in absolute control of everything, so that everything that happens is God's mysterious and loving plan. If we mean that, then the shooter acts out God's plan. That's just terrifying. And if we really do mean that, then God's love is expressed in murderous bullets. If so, then God is the perpetrator of all vile acts. If so, the word *love* becomes meaningless.

But the twisted ideas of God's love don't stop there in this example. It is just as troubling to hear how many people have said that God *abandoned* those children because we have *banished God from our public schools*. For example, in response to the Newtown shooting, former Arkansas governor and presidential candidate Mike Huckabee said, "We ask why there is violence in our schools, but we have systematically removed God from our schools. Should we be so surprised that schools would become a place of carnage?"[5] Huckabee's definition of God requires him to believe we should not be surprised by Newtown. His definition of God abandons those

4. "President Obama's Speech at Prayer Vigil."
5. Blumenfeld, "Tragic Shootings Blamed."

children to murderous bullets because people don't pray in public schools anymore. How puny and petty is the God who would actively withhold love, care, concern, and protection for human beings—children in particular—because there is no public worship of God in public schools? How can *that* be God? It can't be.

It turns out it might not really be a problem with "God" we need to address. Rather, it is our *definition* of God that needs serious attention. What's giving God a bad name is really a false God who goes by many names, with many terrifying definitions. So, let's set out on our journey to end the reign of that false, Tornadic and Murderous God once and for all, so the God of love can shine bright. The first step will be to pick the brain of a cultural commentator and satirist named Stephen Colbert. He will give us the first tool we need so to rediscover the truth that God is powerful love. That tool is the term *truthiness*.

Chapter 2

Truthiness

On Monday, October 17, 2005, the world witnessed the triumphant ascent of comedian Stephen Colbert, the "Troubadour of Truthiness."[1] Colbert's entertaining comedy accomplishes a mission of social commentary meant to make us think. By wholeheartedly and intelligently adopting the fictitious persona of a bombastic right-wing television pundit, Colbert cut directly to the bone, exposing the many layers of rank absurdity in US culture during the first decade of the new millennium. In his own words during the first episode of his *The Colbert Report*, he "presented America with a concept to define our times: truthiness."[2] His satirical presentation of the *way things are* in America begins with that crucial word, *truthiness*. In an April 2008 interview with Susan Jacoby about her book *The Age of American Unreason*, Colbert proposed that his show's premiere date—when he introduced *truthiness* to the world[3]—was the birthday of the *age of American unreason*. Well, we can at least say that's the day we finally had a word to express it.[4]

Truthiness means a divide: usually the preference of "heart" or "gut" to the exclusion of "head" or "mind." To illustrate that divide, Colbert declares that he does not "trust books. They're all fact, no heart."[5] He goes on to say, "we are divided between those who *think* with their head, and those who

---

1. Gladstone, "Troubador of Truthiness."

2. Colbert, *Colbert Report*, season 2, episode 132.

3. Colbert, *Colbert Report*, season 4, episode 53.

4. It seems American unreason has not died. The cover story of *Time Magazine*, on April 3, 2017, was "Is Truth Dead?" It is introduced with an inscription on page 2 that says, "The State of Truthiness: How fact-challenged President Donald Trump delivers deliberate and strategic lies to control the national debate."

5. Colbert, *Colbert Report*, season 1, episode 1.

know with their heart."[6] His most formal definition of truthiness came in a graphic on his Comedy Central program:

> 1 : truth that comes from the gut, not books *(Stephen Colbert, Comedy Central's "The Colbert Report," October 2005)*

> 2 : the quality of preferring concepts or facts one wishes to be true, rather than concepts or facts known to be true *(American Dialect Society, January 2006)*[7]

In other words, truthiness is dangerous because it falsely inflates partial truth, as if it were the whole truth. But, truthiness really *does* require acknowledging that there are such things as facts—unlike the more recent arrival of a "post-truth" world.[8] In an interview on Christmas Day 2016, Stephen Colbert—the real person, two years out of character—reiterates that in *truthiness* facts are at least known to exist, but,

> then there's post-truth, which is not associated with the facts . . . there are no facts. That's truly in a whole new world. That's—that's before God said let there be light. That's absolute chaos. And that scares me, the idea that facts don't exist anymore is actually scary to me, whereas if there are no facts anymore, then there is nothing to agree upon and so we can't agree. You can't build anything.[9]

Truthiness might seem dismal—a genuine divide that needs to be overcome. But, it isn't the chaotic hopelessness of post-truth, which incidentally was Oxford Dictionaries' word of the year for 2016.[10]

It appears that it really is the case that some people are more inclined to feel with their gut, while others are more inclined to think with their head. But, it also seems that within most people a struggle is waged between head and heart, and no one really lives *entirely* in one or the other. Truthiness prevails whenever anyone picks a side and sticks with it, disregarding the requirements of actual reality. That is to say, the truthiness divide among different people is also a divide *within* each of us. For example, some people in the United States are held hostage by the profound feeling that immunizations for children are the cause for the increase in autism. Facts do

6. Ibid. (emphasis mine).

7. Colbert, *Colbert Report*, season 2, episode 156.

8. Indeed, the truth was further assaulted in January of 2017 with the coining of the term *alternative facts*, which, it turns out, are simply *lies*.

9. Dickerson, "Face the Nation Transcript December 25, 2016."

10. "'Post-Truth' Declared Word of the Year."

not back up that feeling. But try telling that to anti-vaccination crusaders. Especially in the case of a conflict or a contradiction, the sway of far more influential feeling often overrules rational thought and facts.

Truthiness Is One-Sided Junk Thought

In his interview with Susan Jacoby, Colbert verifies the derogatory connotation of truthiness when he complains to her: "You describe something called 'junk thought,' where people only know what they want to know, while facts that challenge their beliefs are brushed aside. I believe that's called truthiness."[11] He is right. Truthiness *is* junk thought. And it is junk thought because it is one-sided, leaving out the head by leaving all to the gut. But, another kind of junk thought, or truthiness, resides entirely in the head while omitting the gut. Truthy[12] thought is one-sided junk thought of either variety: gut feelings unverified by cold hard facts, or cold hard facts that don't match up with gut feelings.

Reality is so complex that we need to engage our whole selves together in the complementary arts of *knowing* and *feeling*. Reality is so complex that it cannot be fully expressed with absolute and dogmatic terms. But when people rely on truthy, one-sided ways—*going with the gut*, or *just the facts*—they can fall prey to the illusion of certainty. Minds and hearts alike can become cluttered with petty dogmatisms about important things. Certainty deceives us into believing we have captured the totality of the truth, when we boil vast constellations of ideas down to deceptively simplified propositions. Of course, fully apprehending the whole truth is not possible since *every* knowing and *every* feeling is always partial, and every choice excludes other truths. So, there is always *some*thing truthy (emphasizing either intellect or feeling) about our knowledge. It is always incomplete. But it is only a real problem when we are falsely convinced our truthy view is the whole story.

This one-sided junk-thought approach to reality called truthiness does admittedly have a positive aspect. The accumulation of experience, sensibility, and general notions of how the world works and what people are like should not be immediately ignored. To some degree, we do need to be able to trust our gut.[13] If we can't do that, the world spirals into a kind

11. Colbert, *Colbert Report*, season 4, episode 53.

12. *Truthy* is the adjectival form of the noun *truthiness*.

13. As Colbert says, "Now, I know some of you may not trust your gut yet, but with

of indecipherable and chaotic mystery. The problem is when gut feeling *replaces* other kinds of knowing.

There is also a place for reliance on facts alone, in matters of health and safety, for instance. But simply reversing truthiness, replacing a gut truthiness with a head truthiness, is no better. People should not be fooled into supposing the only truth is a verifiable fact. That can also be truthiness because it is rationality that omits feeling.

Think about someone you love. Now try to express the real depth and wonder of that person in declarative sentences of fact. It cannot be responsibly done because the reality of a human person is too rich and complex for a list of mere facts. But neither can truth be reduced to mere feelings. Authentic truth requires a holistic approach that honors head and heart alike.

Truthiness is the dehumanizing division of the head from the heart and vice versa. It is dehumanizing to ignore half of who we are; dehumanizing to ignore our feeling; dehumanizing to ignore our thinking. If we want to encounter truth, fact and feeling, head and heart require each other for completion. Sure, truthiness can be a first resort gut-check that gives direction, or a fact-check that leads to greater clarity; but we should not be in the habit of dehumanizing ourselves by resorting to truthiness as our last or only resort. We deserve to be wholly human.

---

my help you will." Colbert, *Colbert Report*, season 1, episode 1.

Chapter 3

The Regime
of Divine Truthiness

The focus of this book is how people relate—or don't relate—to the God who is love. While it is clear that Colbert's coining of the term *truthiness* originally shone a light on a primarily sociopolitical divide, its foundational insight is broader and can easily apply to God as well. Even if we haven't thought it out fully, many people may have a gut sense, a heartfelt feeling, that there is a divide between what we *feel* about God and what we *think* about God. And often we don't know what we really think or feel until we say it out loud. When we do so, we sometimes feel vindicated, and sometimes feel, "Wow, that can't be right!" This book takes a close look at some bogus "facts" about God that religions have been peddling for centuries.

Colbert's notion of *truthiness* provides an excellent starting point in this investigation. On his Comedy Central show, Colbert would often recite large portions of the Nicene Creed, the preeminent statement of belief for many Christians. On one such occasion, he concludes by saying, "Now, what I just said is either the complete truth or the Muslims are right, and I'm an infidel."[1] Earlier in the segment, he had declared that he's a Roman Catholic, which he said means he's a member of "the one true faith," and then he fake-apologizes to Islam because "inherent in [his] belief is [their] wrongness," and goes on to say that Islam "better be wrong. I'd hate to think that all those people in the Spanish Inquisition were tortured for nothing."[2] All of these satirical statements are perfect examples of absolutist truthiness. Tongue firmly in cheek, Colbert praises absolutist strains of Islam, and decries strains of Christianity—even the Roman Catholicism promoted by a conservative like Pope Benedict XVI—that seek common ground with

1. Colbert, *Colbert Report*, season 2, episode 148.
2. Ibid.

other religions. He complains, "When Christians try to be ecumenical,[3] we just look weak in our faith."[4] His punch line presses the weak and rigid logic of absolutism to its absurd end, eliciting a knowing laugh from the audience: "If different religions have to agree, let's agree on the one thing we both believe: that the other guy is going to hell."[5]

In November 2011, Colbert's satirical flame burned ever more brightly when he illuminated the shame of truthiness applied to ideas about God. Quoting Leviticus 20:13, which is an Old Testament supposed proof text that seems to demand homosexual men be put to death for having "sexual relations with a man as one does with a woman," Colbert exposes the rank irony of truthiness in that kind of proof-texting: "That's not me, that's God: the all-loving, all-knowing Creator of all things who hates some of them."[6] And it is precisely here that Colbert exposes the devastating effects of truthiness applied to *ideas about God* (i.e., theology). Incoherent and dangerous notions about God, such as the *loving hateful God*, are deadly gibberish called *divine truthiness*.

The term *divine truthiness* needs to be clearly understood. Please do not read it as a positive thing, the way we sometimes use the term *divine*, as in, "This peach cobbler is simply divine." If truthiness is junk thought, divine truthiness is junk thought about God. *Divine truthiness* is a term meant to alert you to the dangers that pour out of wrong and harmful notions about God. The term *divine truthiness* points to dehumanizing half-truths about God/divinity/ultimate reality. Junk thought about God can even be called a "regime" of divine truthiness because there is a long-standing power structure enforcing its decrees in religions and theologies.

The *regime of divine truthiness* works hard to enforce belief in the incoherency of a God who is the *all-loving Creator of all things,* yet who somehow also *hates some of those creations.* That idea is divine truthiness par excellence because it proposes an impossibly conceived God. The theologian David Ray Griffin makes this same point: "just as no amount of evidence can prove the existence of a round square, no amount of evidence

---

3. The term *ecumenical* actually applies to dialogue within Christianity's various denominations, and Colbert mistakenly applies it to what is properly called "interfaith" or "interreligious" dialogue between Christianity and Islam—but his meaning is not lost.

4. Colbert, *Colbert Report*, season 2, episode 148.

5. Ibid

6. Colbert, *Colbert Report*, season 8, episode 19.

can prove the existence of a deity incoherently conceived."[7] The truthy God is incoherently conceived because love cannot mean hate. Insistence on truthy ideas, like love being defined as hate, leads to justifiable atheistic protest. Thoughtful and sensitive theists have much in common with atheists when they join together in revolution against an incoherent and truthy God. And Colbert's satirical coining of the word *truthiness* gives him the ability to demonstrate the truth that the God we have been sold has been *incoherently conceived* in the extreme. When the love of God is depicted as a kind of hatred, it is no wonder that people refuse and flee such a detestable deity. It is time for a regime change.

Truthiness dehumanizes us. Divine truthiness elevates that dehumanization to the level of God. This broken, dismembered, dehumanized condition divides a person's head and heart; divides communities between liberals and conservatives; divides educated and uneducated people; divides enriched and impoverished people. Those and so many other divisions mean we need to be un-broken, re-membered, re-humanized to genuine wholeness.

Satire has power because it uncovers the truth of *how things really are. But, are organized religions up to that same task*? With great hope and expectation, this book looks also to resources within three of those organized religions—Buddhism, Christianity, and Taoism[8]—for the additional tools we need to end divine truthiness and replace it with truth that is whole—holy truth that honors head and heart. Our next step in the journey to end divine truthiness is to provide some definition for the term *love*, so we can with confidence recognize when truthy ideas of God are mangling ideas of love. With Colbert's satirical word truthiness guiding us to see *how things really are*, I hope you will be delighted by the next chapter, where a Buddhist notion for *how things really are* is our launching point for recognizing *bona fide* love.

---

7. Griffin, *Reenchantment without Supernaturalism*, 134.

8. The *T* in Tao and Taoism is pronounced like a *D*, so "Dow" and "Dow-ism" are better pronunciations than resorting to a hard *T* sound.

Part 2

Love

God wills the interdependence of creatures. The sun and the moon, the cedar and the little flower, the eagle and the sparrow: the spectacle of their countless diversities and inequalities tells us that no creature is self-sufficient. Creatures exist only in dependence on each other, to complete each other, in the service of each other.

CATECHISM OF THE CATHOLIC CHURCH, 340

I believe that unarmed truth and unconditional love will have the final word in reality.

REV. DR. MARTIN LUTHER KING, JR.
(DECEMBER 10, 1964, OSLO, NORWAY)

Chapter 4

Buddhist Tathata
(How Everything Really Is)

If we are going to talk about love, we have to know something about relationship. To talk about love, we need to ask, *what is the real nature of
relationships in the world we live in?* We can begin to answer that by appealing to Buddhists, who have a technical term—*Tathata*—for the truth
of how everything interrelates. Because it is an omnipresent reality, it can
be difficult to express *Tathata*, or *how things really are*. The common phrase
"It is what it is" conveys an inkling about Tathata. Trying to express Tathata
means looking for a way to acknowledge what we already know to be true
about the nature of things—even if we have never said it. Jay B. McDaniel
does as good a job as any, explaining Tathata: "'Suchness' is the [English]
translation of the Buddhist word Tathata. It means the as-it-is-ness of
things, the sheer happening of things as they occur on their own terms."[1]
More graphically, he refers to Alan Watts's playful and poetic speculation:

> that the Sanskrit word *tathata* may well have its origins in the
> sounds of babies as they first discover the sights and sounds of
> nature . . . A small child lies in a crib, for example, and her father
> opens a window. The child looks out the window and sees, for the
> first time, softly sprinkling rain. The child says "da-da-da," which,
> Watts speculates, sounds a bit like "tathata." The father thinks
> that she is saying "da-da" or "daddy," but truly she is saying "look-
> look-look, look what is there." She is experiencing the rain in its
> suchness.[2]

That creative approach to Tathata (suchness) should be aligned with Jesus' insight that Yahweh-God is *Abba-Abba*—which is something like

1. McDaniel, *With Roots and Wings*, 50.
2. Ibid., 51.

the English "Dadda-Dadda"—both of which resonate rather like *Tathata*. Similarly, one of Raimundo Panikkar's prayerful asides in the book *Christophany* draws together a feeling of radical dependence, of pure giftedness from the source of everything: "*Abba Pater!* I do not originate my very being, I am a pure gift. I have received everything that I am, including what I define as 'mine.'"[3] Tathata is the *tap-tap-tap* of the rain, and the *da-da-da* of the babbling infant. Pure-gift-ness is the reality of existence, how things really are. Tathata is unalloyed reality. Tathata can never be reduced to mere words and symbols—but that doesn't mean we can't give it our best effort to understand.[4]

Being or Becoming?

So what *is* the reality of things? What is the Tathata of reality? The most basic question is whether Tathata is better described by the concept *being* or the concept *becoming*. The Western Christian mind, formed largely by Thomas Aquinas's reliance on Aristotle, is trapped thinking that *being* has priority over *becoming*. This is problematic because love strongly implies the priority of becoming, since love adapts by becoming something new in each new moment. Love as a process of becoming has been articulated by the writing of Pierre Teilhard de Chardin (a Roman Catholic priest, mystic, and theologian) in his book *Christianity and Evolution*. There, Teilhard suggests we should replace a paradigm of essential completed being with a paradigm of ongoing unification because "we see that from a dynamic point of view what comes first in the world for our thought, is not 'being' but 'union which produces this being.'"[5] Teilhard emphasizes a process of gradual unification, a process of gradual becoming in sharp contrast to the more static category of being, or finished perfection.

The *completed perfection* implied in the category *being* has long been applied to God. This is a problem because literally everything else in existence obviously demonstrates a devastating lack of *completed perfection of being*. If we can instead identify a *process of becoming* that somehow includes God's love, then we may at long last be liberated from the ideology

---

3. Panikkar, *Christophany*, 101.

4. And actually, theologians say the same sorts of things about God: you can't ever fully capture God in your words, symbols, ideas, rituals, or sacraments.

5. Teilhard de Chardin, *Christianity and Evolution*, 227.

that demeans every reality except God. The efforts to overcome truthiness will help us to recognize Tathata, which has to be the truth of love.

While Christians routinely use love language, they are not alone. Jews have the Hebrew word, *hesed*, or loving-kindness, denoting divine love for humanity—even in spite of human fickleness and changeableness. Buddhists have the Pali word *metta*, likewise often translated as loving-kindness. *Metta* also refers to a meditation practice offering unconditional love that makes others' feelings, perceptions, and experiences as important as one's own. But here's the key: loving-kindness must always adapt because the beloved is always changing, always becoming new. That means the love that embraces the beloved must also be in a perpetual relational process of becoming new. The loving-kindness known as *hesed* and *metta* reminds us that love is not some static being. Love, like all relationship, is on the move. Love, like all relationship, is dynamic: the very Tathata of the reality human beings encounter through our tender hearts and bright intellects. Love is the *becoming together* of lover and beloved.

The turning point is the Christian definition of God that says God is love: "Whoever is without love does not know God, for God is love" (1 John 4:8). If God is love, and love is never static, then can we at least be open to the possibility that God really is love? Even if that means God also might not be a static being, precisely because God is love?

Chapter 5

Mutual Becoming

The aim of this book is to end divine truthiness, and to replace it with holistic truth about God's love that is in harmony with God's power. That task requires us to enlarge our vision. It means letting more of reality into our investigation. Of course, it won't be possible to achieve absolute totality of meaning. But it is possible to open our hearts and minds to accept truth from many sources. We can expand our communion with more of the people of Earth. Engaging with perhaps unfamiliar religions and philosophies is a chance to enlarge our humanity. And an enlarged humanity is exactly the opposite of divine truthiness, which dehumanizes and stunts our potential by depleting the communion of head and heart. Dispensing with divine truthiness and replacing it with coherent and inspiring divine truth means re-igniting the awe and beauty and wonder of ourselves and the rest of creation as epiphanies of God and the universe. We are face to face with the simple truth that the cosmic expanse and microscopic intimacy conspire to disclose a deep fellowship whose history originates in a powerful beginning we can scarcely describe, and whose end defies our wildest dreams.

Sulak Sivaraska, Buddhist economist and monk, teaches that *becoming* bonds all creatures together. In fact, the connective power of becoming is the essence of the Buddha's teaching that describes the Tathata of the universe:

> When this exists, that comes to be,
>> with the arising of this, that arises.
> When this does not exist, that does not come to be,
>> with the cessation of this, that ceases. [1]

That linkage of becoming is the mutual arising of all phenomena (*pratitya samutpada* is the Sanskrit term) whereby everything co-becomes in

1. Kiriyama, *21st Century, the Age of Sophia*, 103.

mutuality with every other thing. And this is not only a Buddhist idea. Sivaraksa reminds us: "the interrelatedness of all beings, as expressed in Buddhism, is lived in the traditions of indigenous peoples throughout the world."[2] In fact, if there is anything that approaches a universal wisdom, it is certainly not the artificial separateness of disconnected individuals. The more universal wisdom is something more akin to what Paul F. Knitter calls "this solidarity which links cosmos, humanity, and divinity in a mutuality and interconnectedness in which we are all responsible for each other's well-being."[3]

The truth of Tathata is becoming that is mutual. Mutual means shared. Mutual means together. When becoming among many individuals is described as mutual it means everyone is implicated in the rest by *sharing together* the processes of coming into being. Everything depends on everything else. Tathata's holistic truth, which honors deepest feeling and is verified by rational investigation, might best be called *mutual becoming*. The foundation of all relation, and therefore the foundation of love, is mutual becoming—the Tathata of reality.

In sharp contrast, Western individualistic consumerism demands a worldview of human beings as disparate, separate beings in the midst of a disconnected world. It is an unresolved irony that hyper-individualistic Western culture oversees the rise of economic and technocratic globalism, and comes with tools of instantaneous global communication. Western culture labors to construct systems of artificial interconnection, even while a far more impressive organic interconnectivity is already present. As for religion's response to this, Teilhard genuinely hopes

> theologians will somehow come to realize that, in a universe as organically structured as that of which we are now becoming conscious, a solidarity of man, much closer even than that which they seek in "the bosom of Mother Eve," is readily provided for them by the extraordinary internal cohesion of a world which, all around us, is in a state of cosmo-and anthropo-genesis.[4]

By now, there are enough voices speaking the truth of solidarity of mutual becoming that religions and theologians surely must begin to hear it and take it seriously. Juan Luis Segundo hears: "Only by closing his eyes can a scientist disregard the fact that the 'web' of physiochemical matter

2. Sivaraska, *Wisdom of Sustainability*, 32.

3. Knitter, *One Earth, Many Religions*, 82.

4. Teilhard de Chardin, *Christianity and Evolution*, 211.

shows no clear break in continuity between the most complex molecules of inorganic physics and the most rudimentary molecules entering into the makeup of living cells."[5] Thinking globally, the well-documented insight that comes from human beings travelling in near outer space, seeing the earth as a tiny blue orb suspended in space, has given new vitality to Gaia theory: planet Earth as one total living subject with its own history and an increasingly uncertain future. So, whether we investigate microscopically or macroscopically, it appears there is nothing more fundamentally *solid* than the solidarity that abides in the fellowship of creation.

We have already seen some religious expressions of the sublime observation of interconnection, but Panikkar provides a handy summary of others. His first image is a fundamental Mahayana Buddhist metaphor of the interrelational order of reality, called Indra's Jewel Net. Indra is the king of the gods who has woven an infinite web of strands with a perfectly reflective jewel interlaced into each intersection. At each knot the jewel perfectly reflects every other jewel. So to see all, one only needs to see one, since the process of reflection is infinite and instantaneous. From there, Panikkar adds several other religious versions of this deep wisdom:

> Anaxagoras's . . . "all in all" . . . shivaism's *sarvamsarvatmakam*, Neoplatonism's *speculation*, Aristotle's microcosm/macrocosm, Buddhism's *pratityasamutpada*, Christianity's . . . *perichoresis*, and the mirror (*speculum*) nature of a certain philosophy, as well as the law of karma, the theories concerning the mystical body in so many religions, the *intellectus agens* of Muslim scholasticism, the Enlightenment's universal reason, as well as modern scientific morphogenetics, magnetic fields, and Gaia theory—all seem to suggest a vision of the world that is less individualistic and in which our metaphorical castle does not have to be defended from so many dragons.[6]

The Christian concept of *perichoresis*, refers to the lovely dance of interrelationality within the being of God, who is *three persons* (Trinity) yet also *one* (unity). To this impressive compilation we can add *hsian sheng*, which is the Taoist contribution to this interrelationality that emerged in an ancient dialogue with Buddhism. Alan Watts's helpful introduction to Taoism describes the two sides of reality that mutually require one another, seen through Taoist eyes: *yang* and *yin*:

5. Segundo, *Evolutionary Approach to Jesus of Nazareth*, 5:44.
6. Panikkar, *Christophany*, 61.

The key to the relationship between yang and the yin is called *hsiang sheng*, mutual arising or inseparability. As Lao Tzu put it: When everyone knows beauty as beautiful, there is already ugliness; [23] when everyone knows good as goodness, there is already evil. "To be" and "not to be" arise mutually; Difficult and easy are mutually realized; Long and short are mutually contrasted; High and low are mutually posited . . . Before and after are in mutual sequence. [104c][7]

Of course, *mutual requirement*, *mutual arising*, and *mutual sequence* are ways of indicating the truth that undergirds *mutual becoming*.

There is an idea in the Apostle Paul's Letter to the Galatians that we could call *sow-reaping*. It is the familiar idea that people reap what they sow—in other words, they harvest what they plant. Sow-reaping is a Christian hint toward what Buddhists call *karma*. Sow-reaping points to the truth of how the behavior of one individual impacts the future of that individual, and other individuals, and communities. Sow-reaping is a Christian way of understanding mutuality of becoming through cause and effect. The Apostle Paul instructs,

Make no mistake: God is not mocked, for a person will reap only what he sows, because the one who sows for his flesh will reap corruption from the flesh, but the one who sows for the spirit will reap eternal life from the spirit. Let us not grow tired of doing good, for in due time we shall reap our harvest, if we do not give up. So then, while we have the opportunity, let us do good to all . . . (Gal 6:7–10).

Sow-reaping can be a helpful image to remember how the effects of actions reach into the unfolding of existence for other beings—and how they echo back into one's own becoming.

The integrated view of vast interrelationship is also brilliantly expressed in scientific terms. For instance, not only theologians like Panikkar or religious geniuses like the Buddha, but scientific luminaries like Neil deGrasse Tyson are convinced that "we are all connected to each other biologically, to the earth chemically, and to the rest of the universe atomically."[8]

In my theology classes these days, my students regularly assert as *common knowledge* something called *quantum entanglement*. Basically, when one subatomic particle is linked with another subatomic particle, no matter

7. Watts and Huang, *Tao: The Watercourse Way*, 22–23.

8. goo.gl/VNRzij.

how far apart the particles become, a change to one will always instantaneously happen to the other. It is extraordinary interrelation at its most mind-boggling, both because of the tininess of particles, and because of the irrelevance of extreme distances.

But, even at a more mundane level of observable existence, interconnectivity systems of mutual becoming regularly exceed our ordinary capacity to comprehend. For instance, on September 29, 2012, CommonDreams.org posted to Facebook about a term they had just learned: "trophic cascade." It is a highly suggestive expression because *trophic* usually has something to do with nutrition. In this case, nutrition is made into a metaphor to describe how one organism "feeds" into the life of another organism. Here is what they wrote in their post about *trophic cascade*: "In essence, according to Mary Ellen Hannibal, it simply means: 'The wolf is connected to the elk is connected to the aspen is connected to the beaver.' When we help save them, we save the planet. We save ourselves."[9] Meanwhile, when we overestimate the certainty of our understanding of vast systems of processes, we frequently devastate their subtle interrelations, and ruin their futures.

If the connections in that trophic cascade among those animals and plants are still fuzzy, the following might help. On July 13, 2007, CNN's Anderson Cooper was reporting as part of his "Planet in Peril" series, and introduced the segment this way:

> Earlier this week . . . I was out in the woods on the hunt for a killer at Yellowstone National Park—on the lookout for grey wolves . . . Now the wolves were once near extinction. They're now back at the park and thriving. And while they're killing other animals, they're also bringing new life to the ecosystem . . . If you're lucky enough to see them, they're usually eating something. In this case, a bison . . . The pack will feed on this bison for about 48 hours, but other animals will also enjoy the kill. And this simple fact represents a real change in Yellowstone. The reintroduction of grey wolves to Yellowstone Park began in 1995: a total of 41 wolves were brought back here. Their numbers have increased steadily since then, and they've had a major impact on the ecosystem . . . Doug Smith is the leader of the wolf restoration project in Yellowstone. He takes me to a site of another wolf kill:
>
> [Doug Smith:] This kill is one week exactly.

9. www.facebook.com/commondreams.org.

[Cooper:] After the wolves are done, after the wolves kill the elk, and they eat a certain percentage of it, and then they leave and other creatures come.

[Smith:] Correct. Actually, sometimes simultaneously. The ravens and the magpies arrive instantly. They're right here. Sometimes a wolf's at one end, a raven's at the other end. And then the wolves feed. They can eat up to 20 pounds in one meal. They gorge themselves. And then they typically move off. And then other animals come in: coyotes, black bears, maybe even a grizzly bear.

[Cooper:] And it's not just the animals. The ripple effect extends to the park's plant life, too. This is a stand of willows?

[Smith:] Yeah, it is. And this stand has, uh, grown up in the last ten years since wolves were reintroduced.

[Cooper:] So, why is it that introducing wolves would have an impact on trees, or on bushes?

[Smith:] What we think is happening, is that wolves pose a risk of predation to the elk. Um, and elk eat willows. And so having wolves back on the landscape, after being absent for 70 years, has changed elk behavior.

[Cooper:] Because there are wolves now, the elk have less time to graze, and also there are fewer of them, so the willows are growing. What impact do the willows have?

[Smith:] Right now, Anderson, I'm sitting listening to numerous songbirds in this stand of willow. There's a flycatcher there. I've heard a warbler. Some sparrows. They're all using this stand of willow for this type of habitat is very important to some songbirds.

[Cooper:] And the cascade continues . . . the reintroduction has increased the beaver population in one part of the park ten times over. And beaver dams create ponds, which support waterfowl, and native trout, and so on . . . A single species reintroduced. A dramatic effect on Yellowstone's more than 2 million acres.[10]

With these additions—*quantum entanglement, trophic cascade, cascade,* and *ripple effect*—at this point we have compiled the principal religious and scientific intuition that *the entire adventure of the cosmic journey in every moment is mutual becoming.* In this array of doctrines and observations it is important to clearly recognize the diversity of opinion about the Tathata of nature as unfathomably interrelational and in perpetual flux. One opinion

10. My transcription, based on a personal recording of the broadcast. Cooper's "Planet in Peril" report series anticipated a documentary of the same name, in which he costarred, and which aired on CNN on October 23 and 24, 2007. For more information about the documentary, see the press release at http://www.cnn.com/services/opk/planet.peril/for.html.

does not house them all, but it would be impossible to enumerate all of these expressions of wisdom in every paragraph. "Mutual becoming" is my shorthand for all of the wide variety of expressions of that wisdom of Tathata. These many wisdom traditions conspire to disclose that if *being* means anything, it means *mutual becoming*. Tathata is the power of mutual becoming.

Knitter understands mutual becoming very well: "it is our relating— how we do it and with whom or what—that makes us . . . individuals. We are not 'becomings' but 'becomings-with.' Cut off the 'with' and we cease to exist."[11] This term *becomings-with* reappears in his book *Without Buddha I Could Not Be a Christian*,[12] and helps here because it comes very close to *mutual becoming*. *Becomings-with* recognizes the mutuality that forms individuals in communities.

To be clear, mutual becoming is not just a matter of human relationships. Consider this Zen saying: *When the flower arranger arranges flowers, the flowers arrange her, she arranges her own mind and the mind of the person who enjoys the flower arrangement.* Sure, human relationships are what we sometimes notice most in our conscious experience, but it is easy to overlook that human conscious experience is supported by a breathtakingly vast array of other mutually becoming relations laboring away in obscurity to make that consciousness possible. In this case, the arranger mutually becomes with the flowers; the flowers mutually become with her; the arranger mutually becomes with the viewer, and so on. The distinct and real individuals—human, floral, elemental, etc.—mutually become through their interrelationship with other distinct individuals, forming a solidarity of existence. That's Tathata.

Womanist liberation theologian Monica Coleman says this much more simply: "we do not *have* relationships. We are not discrete selves that can choose whether or not we want to relate to one another. Rather, we *are* relationships."[13] Note that she does not say there is no *me*, *I*, or *we*—of course there are real individuals and real communities. But we are always to be regarded, as the Letter to the Ephesians says, as "members of one another" (4:25), mutually composing one another. Teilhard helps sharpen the definition of mutual becoming by reminding us that however real and distinct an individual is, that individual "is indebted to an inheritance worked upon from all sides—before it ever came into being—by the totali-

11. Knitter, *No Other Name?*, 8.

12. Knitter, *Without Buddha I Could Not Be a Christian*, 10.

13. Coleman, *Making a Way out of No Way*, 55.

ties of the energies of the earth."[14] The communion in which the individual is embedded is a communion of individuals.

Mutual becoming teaches us the value of every particular cosmic epiphany as a subject of its own unique history and future. And it reminds us at every turn that nothing exists all alone. All becoming happens in mutuality and reciprocity. The world of mutual becoming is the only world we know, and it is the kind of world that comes from the God who is love. With all these rich ideas plumbing the true nature of relationships, we can get on with defining love in the mutuality of becoming.

14. Teilhard de Chardin, *Divine Milieu*, 17.

Chapter 6

Love

Teilhard's heart and mind are thoroughly inspired by the idea of evolution. In fact, he announces "the rise (irresistible and yet still unrecognized) over our horizon of what one might call a God (*the* God) of evolution."[1] Talking about the mutual becoming of individuals always means mindfulness about their mutual becoming in their wider environment. His call to recognize the rise of the *God of evolution* is the call to discuss the divine love-relationship that empowers a universe whose Tathata is mutual becoming.

Dionysius the Areopagite, a fourth-century writer, doesn't know the words "Tathata," or "evolution," or the phrase "mutual becoming," but he does speak love language. Dionysius searches for a way to express the deepest, most primordial beginnings of the divine love, and decides on the phrase *the Divine Yearning*. The Divine Yearning is the aboriginal spark of divine love, which is the permanent inclination of lover toward the beloved. He calls the Divine Yearning, as the root of divine being, something *even more divine than love*. The Divine Yearning is the primordial breath of love itself. It is the preexistent urge within the divine love to go beyond itself, to express itself in distinct others who are to be genuinely beloved. And Dionysius doesn't stop there. He observes, "the Divine Yearning brings ecstasy, not allowing them that are touched [by it] to belong unto themselves but only to the objects of their affection."[2] In other words, every individual creature's total existence is a further amplification, a further unfolding of the Divine Yearning love. Creatures composed of the Divine Yearning love, it turns out, are like little reenactors of divine love: they do not belong only to themselves, but they exist to be in intimate and loving relationship with others. God is like that, says Dionysius, and so the world is

1. Teilhard de Chardin, *Christianity and Evolution*, 237.

2. Dionysius the Areopagite, *Dionysius, the Areopagite, on the Divine Names and Mystical Theology*, 105.

a sure likeness and exemplar (or sacrament) of the ecstatic divine love. We are what we are made of. And we are made of love, says Dionysius.

So Teilhard's dream to find the God of evolutionary mutual becoming means to encounter the God whose love is the *basis* for mutual becoming. In other words, the mutuality of becoming that links every individual with the every other individual means that nothing belongs to itself alone. We may dream of going off the grid, but that dream ignores the fact that we compose the grid that makes our coexistence possible.

What Is Love?

"God is love" (1 John 4:8) is the fundamental theological assertion that holistically honors the head and the heart without contradiction. But words have to have meaning. Symbols have to be intelligible. Sadly, there are too many incoherent and meaningless ideas about God, too many examples of divine truthiness, like the one Colbert mentioned where God's love is expressed as hate. The challenge is to harmonize our ideas about God with the definitive statement *God is love*. If God's love starts to sound like hate, violence, retribution, or wrath, then the word love loses its meaning. When that happens, we know we have encountered the regime of divine truthiness. Whatever dismantles divine love into incoherent babble leads to ruin. The most common culprit that spoils divine love is a wrong idea about divine power.[3]

For a Christian, love is absolutely central, in no small part because it is central to the message of Jesus who distills the divine power into the elegant twofold law of love: *love God and love your neighbor as yourself* (Matt 22:36–40). But love is even more than that. We shall see in part 4 that genuine power in harmony with love has been variously expressed in Christian, Buddhist, and Taoist religious languages. The creatures of the world are the children of love. Their firm foundations are love. Their urge toward the future must also be love.

If we want to know something about the divine source of the world, we should be able to investigate the world. Divine love births cosmic love. The house made of wood will be subject to and respond in keeping with qualities

3. Part 3 of this book will walk us through some of the insidious examples of divine truthiness where twisted ideas of power ruin love. Part 4 defines, with the help of Buddhism, Christianity, and Taoism, the sort of power that makes love shine. But we need a clear-eyed view of love, so we can recognize where the theology goes wrong, and see places where power destroys love rather than building it up. This book is leaning toward a definition of love and power where neither impairs the other.

of wood. For example, the wood house will burn because wood burns. The creature made of love will be subject to and respond in keeping with qualities of love. For example, the creature made of love will love, because love loves. The world exists in continuity with its divine source. This is why theology matters. If God's powerful love is mangled into a kind of hate, then we are faced with the horror that we are composed of hateful love. But if God is real love, and God's power is the loving sort of power that expresses itself as a world of love, the horror retreats. We could say the world is the supreme sacrament—the visible aspect of the invisible, powerful divine love.

If God is love, and God is omnipresent, that means divine love is everywhere (see chapter 20, the subsection entitled, "Omnicaritas is the Source of Tathata"). When divine love can be found everywhere, the great news is we really can know something about divinity by knowing something about the world. Therefore, if mutual becoming is the Tathata of reality, the wisest answer is to cut away divine truthiness, and see that the Tathata of the world is the actual imprint, the discernable evidence of powerful divine love on her creation.

If God is love, and we accept as true that we are created in the image of God (Gen 1:26–27), that means we are created in the image of love. So, understanding the truth of love is the best way to know God, and the best way to know our own true nature. Divine love manifests in the world and especially in human life when people gratefully receive, and generously give away the good gifts of existence without conditions, and without calculating the costs. Divine love wells up as human love when empathy expresses itself as unmerited charitable love that expects nothing in return.

If our ideas and symbols of God have any meaning at all, there has to be in them some real correspondence to our experience of them. And when we apply a symbol—like *love*—to God, we have to root it in something real. Roman Catholic theologian Elizabeth Johnson is correct when she says, "the symbol of God functions."[4] When we use the word "love" it has to mean something similar to what we experience as real love. For love to be a *fully functioning symbol* for God, love can't mean hate. To inquire into the meaning of divine love means we need to identify the real characteristics of real love here in the real world. Love defies divine truthiness. So, what are the hallmarks of real love within a reality whose Tathata is vast, breathtaking mutuality of becoming?

4. Johnson, *Quest for the Living God*, 98.

Chapter 7

Love Is Empathy

L ove can't be hate. Love can't mean inflicting violence on another being. Love can't mean the creation of victims. If we want to say God is love, then "love" has to be in some way analogous to the experience of genuine human love. When reflecting on what people mean when they say the word *love*, empathy often surfaces as the chief definition. Empathy is an active and adaptive ability to participate compassionately in another's thoughts and feelings. To have any hope to follow the advice of Jesus to *love the neighbor as the self* will require nothing less than empathetic love. The person who has no ability to feel what you are feeling, no ability to imagine life from inside your skin, has no ability to love you *as you*. He may enjoy something about you that he observes from the outside, but with no sense of empathetic participation, it doesn't seem possible to call that observational enjoyment "love." Now even if that friend should go out of his way to do nice things for you, even very nice things—even very important and necessary nice things—without that shared participation known as empathy, that cannot really be described as "love." Love without empathy isn't love.

In many theologies we meet a bizarre and truthy God whose love is just like that: an empathy-free zone. John B. Cobb, Jr. and David Ray Griffin point to the absurdity that "love is often defined by theologians as 'active good will,'"[1] that is totally devoid of the notion of empathetic compassion. The truthy God who enforces an unthwartable will on powerless creatures is deficient in sympathetic compassion, deficient in empathetic love. How can this bizarre talk of a Father God who is unmoved, unchanged by a creation that rejoices, and unchanged by a creation that suffers—how can that God be love? Even worse, how can that be the God who is *perfect* love? A human parent who acts like that is not "perfect"! A parent—or especially a *God*—"who remained in absolute bliss while their children were in agony

1. Cobb and Griffin, *Process Theology*, 46.

would not be perfect—unless there are such things as perfect monsters!"[2] A God without empathy becomes a *perfect monster* who has the terrifying knowledge of how to harm and destroy us with the most efficiency. It is time to stop contorting divine love into a monstrosity.

Empathy and compassion, the ability to know and feel the experience of another with another, and to really share the experience of another, is at the very core of real love. But, is that too anthropocentric? Since no thing is exempt from the Tathata of mutual becoming, and God is present in and with every thing, as its source, as its power of manifestation, and present as its urge toward a new future, it is necessary to extend the umbrella of empathetic love beyond the human sphere. We can no longer afford the luxury of persisting in our illusions that the human realm is separate from the rest of reality. If we wish to understand the deepest meaning of how the *neighbor is to be loved as the self*, we have to empathetically encounter our whole world as intimately as parts of our bodies, components of our very selves. The neighbor must not be deprived of air to breathe, food to eat, water to drink. Your neighbor is composed of the world—and so are you. Inclusive empathetic love recognizes that we are members of the world, and members of one another. Can we inhabit inclusive empathy like that?

If we look carefully, we see that there is a rudimentary form of God's empathetic love in the most basic of creatures. Everything has real relation to every other thing in the mutuality of becoming. Human love, or empathy, is a further elaboration of this basic dynamic of mutual becoming in the ongoing social construction of every creature. Now, since the world is a reflection of divine love, then divine love must mutually and empathetically participate in some way in the world. So, empathy, which is a necessary component of love in the world, must also be a necessary component of love in God.

When divine generosity is over-emphasized, an important, though usually neglected aspect of empathetic divine love is God's receptivity. One reason it makes ultimate sense for God's love to be able to not only give but also receive has to do with eternal salvation. A God who has no empathy is one who cannot be permeated by the suffering or joy of this world. That would be a truthy God, devoid of the empathetic love we need. But, a God who empathetically participates in our experience receives our experience into the divine life, and can *in-spire us*, or *place into us the breathing Spirit* of empathetic love.

2. Ibid., 47.

Chapter 8

Empathy Is Love as Mutuality
(Solitude and Solidarity)

Empathy is the mutuality of participation in one another's existence. So, empathy requires real, fully centered individuals, each with their own sacred solitude. *Solitude* means the wholesome distinctiveness of the self, the healthy boundaries of the individual, and is meant to stand in contrast to unwholesome loneliness, and isolation. The sacred solitude of an individual makes empathy possible, because empathy requires a real communion or solidarity among real individuals. Solidarity means the wholesome unification among individuals, and is meant to stand in contrast with unhealthy collectivism that erases distinctiveness. There has to be a sacred space for the individual to be itself. But there is also a sacredness to the shared space of solidarity. It is this subtle and necessary interplay of individuals and community that makes everything possible. In human terms, empathy is possible because I am a *me* and you are a *you*. My *me* has its own sacred solitude. Your *you* has its own sacred solitude. But empathy is also only possible because you and I together are also a *we*. There is no such thing as a totally separate individual. Everything is socially created. Every creature is a construction of a relative infinity of causes and conditions. Every existence is implicated in every other existence.

One dynamic tension in empathy lies between these two demands: the demand toward unification with others, and the demand toward uniqueness from others. Both are required. Total union with the rest (or even one other) means the end of the individual. It means a kind of death. Meanwhile, total separation, the ruination of bonds of mutuality, is also the end. It is also a kind of death. Genuine empathy means the necessary, distinct integrity of solitude in each real individual. And genuine empathy means the necessary, unified integration of solidarity in the community of individuals. Empathy is sympathetic participation in the other, a blessed integrity or solitude for each, and a blessed integration or solidarity where neither is subsumed into the other.

Love is only empathy when it happens between (at least) two real subjects. So there must be real individuals who have real distinction, real integrity. The distinction and integrity of each real individual are the building blocks for sacred solitude. An individual with a wholesome integrity, a sacred solitude, meets another individual with wholesome integrity and sacred solitude. Empathetic love means that those individuals cannot remain totally separate. Together those two individuals create community in its smallest form. Together they mutually affect each other by bonds of integration. The bonds of integration among members with their own integrity are the building blocks for sacred solidarity.

Love that is genuine is empathetic love, reaching its highest form in the solitude of individuals within the solidarity of community. The mutuality of empathetic love flourishes when solitude and solidarity are held in balance.

Chapter 9

Empathy Is Love as Reciprocity (Gratitude and Generosity)

This definition of love envisions empathy in another of its most important respects: authentic empathy can't be unidirectional. Because empathetic love is interrelational and mutual, it must in some sense go "both ways" between at least two—me and you—which is really three—me, you, and we—and must be a dynamic and authentic reciprocity. Reciprocity means there is a flow in love between giving and receiving. Reciprocity means there is a breathing of love that exhales (gives) and inhales (receives). So, the reciprocal aspect of love is part and parcel with the mutuality of love: individuals in communion form integrity of individuals by give and take, and form integration of communion by the same dynamics of give and take. No one gets left out of genuine empathetic love.

But, does reciprocity make sense when we talk about *divine* love? After all, it is one thing to say that God impacts a person. Even divine truthiness agrees with that. There seems to be no trouble expressing how God *gives* to creatures. What gets hard for folks to express is how God can *receive* anything from creatures. Erroneous ideas about the stunted divine love of a God who needs nothing make some people struggle to envision a way in which any creature can affect God. No receptivity means no reciprocity. The God who cannot receive from creatures is a divine love without any empathy. And without empathy, love isn't really love.

The biblical notion of God's love for creatures does include some sort of reciprocity, a genuine *give and take*. The Lutheran theologian Paul Tillich finds in the biblical portrait of God what he calls "free reciprocity between God and man [which] is the root of the dynamic character of biblical religion."[1] The biblical God is not some distant omni-absent entity.

1. Tillich, *Biblical Religion*, 80.

If God really is love, we shouldn't be surprised to meet the God of the Bible, whose love is expressed in reciprocity through real relationship. After all, if God cannot receive anything into the divine life, then God couldn't ever really be receptive to the cries of the Hebrews in Egypt. But in Exodus we meet the God who does listen, hear, and act—empathetically receiving into Godself the suffering of the people. And the evidence of empathy is that God takes action to remove the suffering. We meet the God who is not indifferent to the sufferings of the people. And it is that reception of the people's suffering that transforms God's plan and has a real impact on the future for the Hebrews. God receives the request and gives the aid. The people give the request and receive the aid. That's real reciprocity.

There can be a real and empathetic interrelation between God and us, without the need to worry that reciprocity implies that we are on the same level as God. The Hebrews don't have to be equal to God to enter into a genuine give-and-take relationship with God. People can still be people. God can still be God. But the genuine reciprocal relationship transforms the meaning of everything by giving real meaning to love.

The hard part here is if we think God has the kind of power that is unthwartable. One of the truthy notions from part 3 of this book is the big idea of God's omnipotence. It is one of those barely analyzed truisms people often think must be true. It is a truthy quagmire to say God has all the power, so anything that happens has to be what God wanted to happen, which means suffering is God's fault, and so is any decision to stop or perpetuate suffering. Let's hope we can glean the truth that God is not impervious to sufferings without insisting that those sufferings are also the will of God.

One way out of that truthy quagmire for many Christians is to reason that divine love must be something like Christ's love. That impulse is a helpful starting point, because Christians assert that Jesus is God incarnate, God enfleshed, God with a body. The Gospel stories of Christ demonstrate that Jesus encountered everyday people in his earthly life. In fact, he hangs out with some of the lowest of the low in human status. In these relationships the Gospels recount "a reciprocity to the love that is given by Jesus. He gives, seemingly unendingly, but he also receives in a way which is so simple that it often escapes our notice,"[2] says Marjorie Suchocki. When we forget the human Jesus who exemplified reciprocal empathetic love, love that gives as well as receives, we may distort divine love, and think it receives nothing. But what if divine love *is* like Jesus' love, even in receiving?

2. Suchocki, *God-Christ-Church*, 95.

Jesus, whom Christians call the divine Son of God, is the minister who is also the *recipient* of ministry. He is the *receiver* of love. He is the *receiver* of tenderness. Admittedly, he is also the *receiver* of animosity, and the *receiver* of torture. His friendships are real friendships, with real reciprocity, real give, real take, real empathy, real mutuality, and real love.

Reciprocity is the fact of both giving and receiving, which makes love genuinely love. When we think about empathetic love's reciprocity, we can see it requires both relinquishment (giving) *and* reception (getting). In human terms, a supposed love that takes and takes and takes and never gives is a distortion of love that creates suffering by its extreme selfishness. Think again of the breathing metaphor: only inhaling is no way to live, and is literally unsustainable. But the opposite is also true: a supposed love that only gives and gives and gives but never receives anything is a distortion of love that creates suffering by the depletion of the giver. Back to breathing: only exhaling is also no way to live, and is literally unsustainable. A healthy rhythm of give and take, of exhale and inhale, is a model for empathetic reciprocity. As St. Francis teaches, *it is in giving that we receive.*

Meanwhile, *bona fide* love flourishes when mere receiving blossoms into gratitude, and mere relinquishment blossoms into generosity. Both are required. And beyond that, gratitude and generosity are only possible for individuals in community who have the integrity of sacred solitude, and the integration of sacred solidarity. Love means the sacred solidarity of individuals is only possible in a genuine mutuality of solidarity and communion. Love means dynamic give and take lived in reciprocal generosity and gratitude. That is the language of genuine empathetic love. If our description of the God who is love does not entail the necessary components of empathy—generosity, gratitude, solitude, and solidarity—then that cannot really be called God because it cannot really be called love.

And this brings the discussion right up to the precipice where we can survey the landscape ahead. The coming terrain is littered with examples of divine truthiness. But, once we're free of the truthy God, we can celebrate wholesome divine love and wholesome divine power, which sustain each other. To heal means to make whole, so the God who is love is the God who heals the divide of our hearts and minds. Healing requires tender care and loving patience that empowers both the feeling of the heart and the knowing of the head. The task before us is to contribute to the healing of many truthy divides. So the next step is to identify some varieties of divine truthiness—junk thought about God—so together we can build wholesome and holy truth that heralds the end divine truthiness.

Part 3

Divine Truthiness

...we must obey Him at all times that He may never become the angry father who disinherits his sons, nor the dread lord, enraged by our sins, who punishes us forever as worthless servants for refusing to follow him to glory.

RULE OF ST. BENEDICT, PROLOGUE 6-7

. . . a tyranny sincerely exercised for the good of its victims may be the most oppressive.[1]

C.S. LEWIS

Freedom to Question the Truthy God

God is love, and love is powerful. But what we have said about genuine empathetic love must not be forgotten. Love is love when it is empathy marked by mutuality and reciprocity. Love is love when it allows unique individuals to exist in healthy relationships and communion. Love is love when giving and taking are kept in a balance of healthy reciprocity. Now that we understand the real meaning of empathetic love, we can no longer pretend to accept the false and truthy God, whose love is incoherent because it acts like hate.

1. goo.gl/lBi3wP.

The atheists, agnostics, and humanists among us rightly take a stand against harmful ideas about God in which divine power depletes or removes divine love. Certainly most atheists take the stand that there can be no such thing as God no matter how we define God, and they must certainly have the freedom to take that stand. That said, it is not difficult to hear in many atheist criticisms a protest against the genuinely hateful things that are so often wrongly called "God." Frankly, it is hard not to share those same complaints. But those horrors aren't actually God. And we should be able to discuss our shared outrage against the truthy God. My stance is that just because that hateful, deplorable mess isn't God doesn't mean there can be no God at all. We can build an alliance between theists and nonbelievers if we can find the basis for common ground. Not all theists will take that approach, however. So how do people who believe in God reply to the criticisms? What are the alternatives to doubling down on the inherited definitions of God? One option I choose is to say the "God" against whom atheists protest, the "God" about whom agnostics are unwilling to make any definitive claim, and the "God" out of whose shadow humanists wish to engage the fullness of their existence is nothing but *the truthy God and not actually God at all.*

Theologians are people who study God and religion in a systematic way. They are not always careful in what they say. It is easy to get so immersed in the subject that they think everyone thinks as they do. It is also fairly common to hear theologians say things like *everyone believes in some god or another.* Or *everyone has a sense of the highest good or the highest power, or the highest value, and what they really mean by that is god.* This is the sort of talk that makes it hard to have conversations with atheists. So it is not helpful to make those kind of sweeping statements. But, the fact is a majority of people still do believe in the concept of God or in gods—even if they don't exactly agree on the definition.

If someone's definition of God is really the truthy God (whose love is hate, expressed in violence and punishment, and who creates victims), then this book may feel like a strong stand against God in general, because I'm saying *that can't possibly be God.* More, we can't keep insisting that people in other religions need to conform their view to the truthy God with its hateful and violent tendencies. Rosemary Radford Ruether calls cultural or religious claims to "a monopoly on religious truth . . . an outrageous and absurd religious chauvinism."[2] We need the freedom to ask: What if these

2. Ruether, "Feminism and Jewish-Christian Dialogue," 141.

defined traits of God as they have been dogmatized through millennia in a kind of majority report, really don't have much to do with God at all? In that case, the truthy God whose love is hate, whose power destroys, whose will inflicts suffering, and whose commandment creates victims should be protested by smart, passionate atheists . . . and protested, perhaps even more zealously, by smart, passionate theists!

If religious folks are going to be able to engage the rational and passionate critiques of atheists, agnostics, and humanists, it's imperative to first understand what makes them say what they say. It is imperative to understand the troubling and deplorable portrait of God. It is time to consider the forces of distortion that have produced so many misshapen views of God and humanity. But that means we must be permitted the freedom to question, doubt, and distrust some inherited dogmas. This questioning can become uncomfortable and feel like a kind of heresy. But the truth is we *should* critique and distrust the authority of traditional teachings if they are flawed. It's possible to learn to trust intellect, alongside a trust of gut sense. The best guide is heartfelt feeling united with rational thought. That's how to overcome the regime of divine truthiness.

Please understand: by no means do I reject all authority and wisdom. Far from it. I think it is a mistake to ignore the vast, sublime array of wisdom, religious, scientific, and philosophical traditions. But, the task is to honestly evaluate the teachings about God that have been enforced over millennia in an oftentimes-authoritarian process of dogmatic insistence. But let's not just replace one dogmatic certainty with another. An honest, open approach will yield a more significant and more satisfactory minority report whose messages come from many sources, yet with an astonishing harmony.

We cannot ever say enough about a past littered with atrocities committed by the most faithful, most well-intentioned people. And current events indicate no slowing in the proliferation of atrocities. So, the urgency of the task is great. Though urgent, the work to end divine truthiness requires the careful and delicate handling of precious threads. Some threads are tainted, and we need to identify them, so we can leave them behind. But other threads are alive with holistic truth. We need those. If we wish to weave a beautiful, true garment, we will need to know what to include, and what to leave out.

Chapter 10

Theology, Theological Anthropology, and the Image-Imitation Dynamic

When someone supposes God might be real and might be important, *what she thinks of as God* really matters. We are back to the question: What does she mean by the word *God*? It seems like no two people really agree on everything—ever—least of all the meaning of the word "God." Still, we have that word. And everyone thinks they know what someone else means when they use it.

Much to the righteous consternation of many atheists, Tillich observes that there is no person who does not have a god, because everyone has an *ultimate concern*. He argues, we all have some*thing* that concerns us ultimately (i.e. our "god"). In his *Systematic Theology* he explains it this way:

> "God" is the answer to the question implied in man's finitude; he is the name for that which concerns man ultimately. This does not mean that first there is a being called God and then the demand that man should be ultimately concerned about him. It means that *whatever concerns a man ultimately becomes god* for him, and conversely, it means that man can be concerned ultimately only about that which is god for him.[1]

It is unhelpful and insulting to write off the thoughtful grievances of atheists and humanists, because there is so much about the truthy God that demands real rebellion. And they have a right to think what they want to think. But, what *is* helpful from Tillich is the warning against equating *ultimate concern* with the God whose dogmatic traits have been decided by the religious traditions. Sure, *ultimate concern* can mean God—but it simply cannot mean that *fake God*. In spite of replacement phrases, Tillich *does* want to keep the word *God* (and so do I), since there is no one who

1. Tillich, *Systematic Theology*, 1:211 (emphasis mine).

really worships or prays to those replacement abstractions—and there are a lot of them: *ultimate reality, holy reality, ultimate concern*, and even something like John Hick's *the real*, or Cobb and Griffin's *the really real*. There are benefits of hanging on to the term *God*—but *only if we can have a say* in what we mean by it. It will not be sufficient to merely accept the *truthy God*. But, for clarity, we need three key concepts in hand: *theology, theological anthropology*, and the *imitation of God*.

Key Concept 1: Theology (Theologies)

Theos means *God*, and *-logy* means *words*—so, theology is basically the words we say about God. To be fair, all theology intends to be *true* words that are spoken in a *true* way about the *true* God. But, to think theology is a singular monolith presents a problem when one particular brand of theology is the loudest and the most evident to the masses. The predominance of certain theological positions gives the unfortunate impression that there is in fact *one singular theology*—i.e., the prominent evangelical or fundamentalist Christian theology that dominates contemporary American discourse. Prominent proponents (for example, John Hagee, Joel Osteen, Rick Warren) of that *theology*, those *words about God*, have huge followings, and sell lots of books. They are the contemporary perpetuators of the dominant theology. No doubt, those writers and so many others who share their views believe that their theology is true—and that is part of what makes it theology, and not merely religious opinion or religious studies.[2] But, no matter its prominence or its sincerity, one strain of *theology* can never exhaust our *words about God*. Not even the theology in this book.

Actually, the term *theology* should probably not be used in the singular, since there are likely as many *theologies* as there are people who think about God. But, admitting this diversity makes the work harder because, rather than ignoring it, we will have to take especially careful account of the dominant theology. It can't be merely ignored. But neither can we blindly shoot it down. Our stance has to be open to refuting it, but it also has to be open to accepting whatever *is* good and true.

Simply switching from one one-sided truthiness to another will not do. A genuine encounter with divine love requires a *wholes*ome, *healed*,

2. *Religious studies* means scientific, objective study of religion or divinity, and the response to divinity, from a dispassionate outsider's perspective—whereas theology is study of the same topics, but from an insider's view.

holistic—a *holy* approach. The holistic truth approach immediately discovers that what we say about God (theology) cannot be separated from what we say about human beings (anthropology)—and that leads us to the next key concept, *theological anthropology.*

Key Concept 2: Theological Anthropology

One of the key theological questions asks what it means to be a human person. One of the best answers to that complex question can be found in the scandalously named book *The Myth of Christian Uniqueness,* edited by John Hick and Paul Knitter. Among many high-quality essays is one written by Gordon D. Kaufman, who outlines in remarkable fashion the various options available to us as we investigate the many ways human life can be understood:

> . . . as a journey through hazardous territory where one might encounter wild beasts and evil monsters as one sought to get to the safety of home; . . . as participation in a great warfare between the forces of light and the forces of darkness . . . as responsible citizenship in a quasi-political order, the kingdom of God; or as but one stage in a never-ending transmigration of the soul from one form of life to another . . . as a soul fallen out of its proper home in heaven above and become trapped in a physical body from which it must find some way to escape. Or . . . the very sense of self or soul might be regarded as an illusion, as the product of ignorance, the veil of *maya*, which right insights can dispel, thus dissolving the key deep human problems that arise out of this false consciousness. Or . . . a product of the accidental collocation of material atoms, or of blind evolutionary process that could just as well have gone in other directions and formed other patterns.[3]

Wow. To be human must be a remarkable thing indeed to amass such a wide array of possible interpretations. Admittedly, it is a bit difficult to tease apart whether we tell the story and live into it, or we live it and describe it. Likely both happen. One thing becomes clear: there is no one, simple, unified meaning behind the deceptively simple utterance of the words *human, human being,* or *person.* Human reality is as widely interpretable as other complex realities.

3. Kaufman, "Religious Diversity, Historical Consciousness," 7.

Confucians view being human as an intensification of that universal Tathata in a world of mutual becoming. So, Confucians say human being is really human co-being with other humans. If there is anything like a human self, it is a swirling hub of interrelationships. The Confucian name for the swirling-hub-of-relations human person is *jen*, symbolized by the combination of the Chinese characters for *two* and *human*.[4] Alan Watts explains, "at the head of all virtues Confucius put, not righteousness . . . but human-heartedness (*jen*), which is not so much benevolence, as often translated, but being fully and honestly human."[5] *Jen—co-humanity*—is true to Tathata. Since humans are produced from the world of mutual becoming, *jen* should come as no surprise because the insight of mutual becoming teaches that everything—not only humans—is mutually composed of interrelations. Being really means mutual becoming, or we could say co-becoming. Humanity really means co-humanity. A human is always a co-human. Each person's status as a subject is really interdependent on other subjects. The African idea of *ubuntu* comes close to *jen*. In July of 2003, as part of the University of Minnesota's Great Conversations series, Archbishop Desmond Tutu spoke to us of *ubuntu*, which means *I am because we are*. Co-humanity, *jen*, and *ubuntu*: these are deep and beautiful expressions of the mutual becoming that is the very heart of humanity. They are expressions of an interrelational anthropology rooted closely in the Tathata of mutual becoming.

Image of God

But, is there a Christian way to define humanity in light of God by reference to ideas like *jen* and *ubuntu*? It may be possible to find an analogue in the idea called the *image of God* (*imago Dei*, in Latin). Christianity's teaching about the image of God is that humans are called to live as we are created: in the *image of God* (Gen 1:26–27). But what does that mean? Does it mean we "look" like God—that God has a face with human features like eyes and a nose? Probably not. The image of God is typically identified with human *traits* we like to boast about, such as free moral agency, intellect, and dominion over creation. The claim is that at least to some degree these are "shared" characteristics with God. This is where we can begin to see

4. Watts and Huang, *Tao: The Watercourse Way*, 82–83.
5. Ibid.

how theology is embedded in anthropology—the intertwining of the two is precisely the meaning of the term *theological anthropology.*

For a specifically Christian theological anthropology—one that hints at ideas like *jen* and *ubuntu*—that believes humans are created in the image of God, we can look to the relatedness of God as carefully expressed over the centuries in the doctrine of the *Trinity.* The Father, Son, and Holy Spirit, the God of the loving dance of mutuality and reciprocity of three-in-one persons within Godself, is the God in whose image Christians profess to be created. Just as in Christian terms the *Trinitarian God* is permanent inter-relatedness, humans are also permanent interrelatedness. God is relational. Humans are the image of God's relational being.

Image of God and Image of the World

Theologian Jürgen Moltmann agrees about relationality, but expands that idea, and in so doing he offers the helpful suggestion of how we might best position theological anthropology: ". . . before we interpret [human-ity] as *imago Dei*, we shall see [humanity] as *imago mundi*"[6] (image of the world). To be created in the image of the world means we are members of a worldwide fellowship in solidarity and communion with every creature, great and small. Moltmann draws heavily on the first creation account of Genesis,[7] and observes that it is absurd to believe humans are separate from the world. In fact, "as the last thing to be created the human being is also dependent on all the others."[8, 9] Moltmann wants us to see that the world full of creatures does not emerge from us: it is the other way around. In fact, I would add that the word *human* is a metaphor for the fact that we come up from the earth. You probably know the word *exhume*, which means to unearth, because the root *hum* means earth. We *hum*ans are *earth*lings. So, sure, humans are created in the image of God, but *hum*ans are *also* crea-tures in the image of the world. It is healthy to show reverence for both of

6. Moltmann, *God in Creation*, 186.

7. In case the reader is not already aware, please know that in the first few chapters of the book of Genesis there are two distinct narratives of the creation of the universe, including the earth and its inhabitants. It is tempting to fuse the two stories together, but to do that obscures much richness of history and meaning.

8. Moltmann, *God in Creation*, 187.

9. The second creation narrative in Genesis flips the order: humans are created first, rather than last.

those parents. And it is a way for a Christian to see how we participate in universal Tathata.

If people really are made in the *image of God*, it is only because they are also made in the *image of the world*. People are continuous with the rest of the creation, which is continuous with its originating source. This line of thought leads right back to the insightful dogma in Christianity that sees God as utterly relational: Trinity. Trinity means God's internal life is love in reciprocity and mutuality forever dancing in genuine relationship. What a discovery on behalf of loving empathy. What does this mean for the conversation here? It is the delicate and monumental realization that the universe of mutually becoming relationship is a clear reflection of the Trinitarian God, whose energetic and powerful love is relational through and through. People are the image of the God whose internal life is the effusion of loving relationality. Acknowledging that people are truly created in the image of the relational world *and* truly created in the image of the relational God is wholesome theological anthropology. And this way of articulating a theological anthropology of humans created in the image of God is a close cousin to *jen* and *ubuntu* anthropologies.

Key Concept 3: The Image-Imitation Dynamic

Because of the ambiguity of the word *God*, we must be so careful about the meaning of God in the claim that humans are created in the image of God. Bishop John Shelby Spong laments that the gods people have worshipped have often reportedly acted "in the very worst manner of human behavior,"[10] and this does not exclude the Christian God. What if by "God" you mean a God who sends tornadoes, shooters, illness, acts of terrorism, war, untimely death and more as punishments, or "tests"? What if by *God* you mean a monster? Is that the image in which people are created? Getting right to this point, Colbert recently quipped (on his CBS program) about the disheartening notion of God as an omni-absent ruler: "A father's job is to be distant, authoritative, and never quite pleased. That way the children can eventually understand God."[11] That is such a sad statement, but it clearly shows the link between our theology and our theological anthropology. But we don't have to despair because good theology can avoid divinely approved human authoritarianism. Good theology can lead to

10. Spong, *Why Christianity Must Change or Die*, 47.

11. Colbert, *The Late Show*, season 2, episode 157.

good theological anthropology. But, this all matters because of the next key concept: the human impulse toward conformity with, or imitation of, God. Paul Sponheim thinks "we seek to live into the image of God," and "we seek to imagine a world still being created by God,"[12] which means imagining ourselves as still being created, too.

Already in the basic theological anthropology there is evidence of that desire to *live into the image* of the God in which one believes. It is not strange that many people have the desire for their lives to embody the divine truth they hold dear. Apart from that, we might shrug and say *so what?* about theological anthropology. At its best, theological anthropology gives a sense of meaning and responsibility to human beings as ambassadors of divine love in creation. At its worst, if words about God amount to incoherent monstrosities then we conveniently give divine permission to the worst behaviors. So this can be tricky business.

Elizabeth Johnson's important insight for our consideration is her oft-repeated phrase "the symbol of God functions"[13] (see chapter 6). In a way, that is not far from Tillich's assertion that "God" is really a person's *ultimate concern* (see the first page of this chapter), which functions with real effects. Johnson's worthy agenda is to bring light to the terrible ways the *male* symbol of God has functioned to identify God as literally male, and how it has provided cover for male dominance in society, and perpetual demotion of women. That important concern will be treated to a greater extent in chapter 16, but for now we cannot overstate the importance of her insight, *the symbol of God functions.*

When the symbol of God is endowed with a certain theology, the particular characteristics of that theology take on an extreme urgency as soon as we make the accompanying declaration that human beings are created in the image and likeness of *that* God with *those* particular traits. The specific theology becomes decisive once it is tied to human self-understanding because that specific theology will determine just what human characteristics are regarded as godlike, and just what human characteristics are regarded as contrary to God. Great care must be taken to define the term "God" in the phrase "the image of God," because it comes with the urge—even the *command*—to imitate *that* God. I call this the *image-imitation dynamic.*

In our conscious lives we are faced with real choices among alternatives. We are faced with *real freedom* to strive toward the values we believe

---

12. Sponheim, *Love's Availing Power*, 8.

13. Johnson, *Quest for the Living God*, 98.

in. Of course there are competing values, but because "God" functions as the symbol of highest concern, God represents the goal to which humans who do believe in God strive to conform. In that spirit, Moltmann draws a direct connection between theological anthropology and theology: "if humans are 'God's [image],' then they must strive to conform to their God and to be like their God."[14] That *strive to conform* is the image-imitation dynamic.

Cobb and Griffin have described this image-imitation dynamic by pointing out the human "religious drive to correspond with the really real, and to accentuate those dimensions of our existence which we perceive as connecting us with the depths of reality,"[15] which means *God*. Because that is so, our theology makes all the difference. If we have a distorted sense of God, and we think being like that distorted God is what it means to be fully human, then *that* is what we will strive to enact. Are we striving to be like the true God, or like a truthy God? Kenneth Leech warns that "if people work with a wrong view of God, the more religious they become the worse it will get, and it would be better for them to be atheists."[16] Susan Simonaitis expresses her own struggles to be a teacher who reflects a true image of God with the terminology "the God I practice."[17] In other words, who she perceives God to be will be the *God she strives to put into action,* to practice, to imitate. By offering a few historical examples, Lesslie Newbigin writes of the importance of our theology, and how it will impact our actions:

> Think of the Christ of the Byzantine mosaics, a kind of super Emperor, the Pantocrat; Christ of the medieval crucifix, a drooping, defeated victim; the Christ of liberal Protestantism, an enlightened, emancipated, successful member of the bourgeoisie; or the Christ of the liberation theologians portrayed in the likeness of Che Guevara.[18]

The implications are manifold: if God is an emperor, then human beings most like God must be imperial; if God is a defeated victim, then human suffering must somehow be justifiable; if God is a member of the bourgeoisie, then the status quo of human-as-consumer must be protected; or if God is a violent revolutionary, then human brutality claims divine endorsement.

14. Moltmann, "God Is Unselfish Love," 118.

15. Cobb and Griffin, *Process Theology*, 21.

16. Leech, *Spirituality and Pastoral Care*, 50.

17. Simonaitis, "Teaching as Conversation," 104.

18. Newbigin, *Foolishness to the Greeks*, 8.

To be sure, often, *image of God* theological anthropology means to say that humanity's creation in the image of God describes the essence of humanity. But the practical application resides in our theology, our understanding of God, because human beings who are committed to a particular God with particular characteristics will undoubtedly "accentuate those dimensions of [their] existence which [they] perceive as connecting [them] with"[19] the God they discern. The type of God we define matters totally, because that is the God we imitate.

In all these cases, the presumption is that theological anthropology is not *only* some kind of static, matter-of-fact ontological status. Instead, these authors are indicating by their use of these phrases—*the symbol of God functions*; *the desire to be in harmony; striving to conform to their God and to be like their God; religious drive to correspond with the really real and to accentuate those godlike dimensions of our existence*; and *the God I practice*—that there is a real interaction among operative theology, human self-understanding, and human behavior. Because humans are not robots enslaved to absolute determinism, but instead are beings of authentic freedom, feelings, and thoughts, theology must be carefully constructed because it informs our actions. Theology is hugely consequential since it will be enacted with an urgent striving to conform to God, to perform the will of God, to *imitate* God.

In Matthew's Gospel we see Jesus' own friends asking him how they should pray to God the Father—and his advice was that they must ask that through them God's will shall be done on earth (6:10). If that is the case, then everything depends on what the will of that God is. The two are closely linked: a merciful God probably wills mercy; a vengeful God probably wills revenge. This dynamism of theology, theological anthropology, and the urge to imitate God[20] is the seldom-named, but very important image-imitation dynamic.

We must remain mindful of just what we are imitating. It is so easy to fall into the trap of creating God in our own image. Many have done it. To oppose divine truthiness, we need a keen sensitivity for any so-called divine characteristic that is actually a dangerous elevation of human foibles, failings, and futilities. We need to ask, for instance: Is God vengeful, or is it truer to say that humans are vengeful and we are just fabricating divine

---

19. Cobb and Griffin, *Process Theology*, 21.

20. Some Christians may be familiar with a similar notion, *imitatio Christi*, the imitation of Christ, indicated by the popular acronym WWJD? (What Would Jesus Do?).

permission to seek revenge? But, you may ask, *what about God's vengeance in the Bible?* All I can say at this point is this inclination to elevate human vices to the status of God is not a recent invention. Can we be open to the possibility that the enthronement of the worst human vices, like vengeance, is a divine truthiness (junk thought about God) that rears its ugly head *even in the Bible?* The good news is we don't have to repeat past mistakes. With the conceptual tools of truthiness, love, theology, theological anthropology, and the image-imitation dynamic firmly in hand, we can now explore some examples of divine truthiness. We begin with the truthy notion of the Imperial God and the Cult of Onlyness.

Chapter 11

The Imperial God and
the Cult of Onlyness

I s it possible for us to think about God without resorting to misleading ideas that God is some kind of king or emperor? After all, the *Kingdom of God* was a favorite symbol for Jesus' own teaching. How do we engage in an earnest critique of the God of truthy theism, when we have this inkling that God has to be ultimately in powerful control—the kind of power exercised by kings and emperors—while at the same time we know well that kings and emperors seldom have reputations for love and mercy? Words matter. Symbols function. When we know that love means empathy, the point of breakdown is the clash of the claim that God is love with the incompatible claim that God functions like an autocratic ruler of the universe. Acknowledging this incompatibility begins the process of undoing idolatrous notions of God, called divine truthiness.

The first of these potential idolatries that lead to the divine truthiness of the Imperial God is the captivating idea of divine oneness. The logic of empire, after all, demands that one and only one way is the correct way. Empire conquers difference and absorbs it, erases its distinctiveness, and insists on uniformity. Empire seeks death to minority consciousness. Perhaps it is due to lazy agreement with the feeling that "the world can no more have two summits than a circumference can have two centers,"[1] that throughout history we have so many set notions of God as the Imperial Ruler, which, as Alfred North Whitehead correctly says, is "the most natural, obvious, idolatrous theistic symbolism."[2] Teilhard takes it as axiomatic that "there is, in reality, *only one* humility in the world, *one* loving-kindness, *one* sacrifice, *one* passion, *one* laying in the tomb, *one* resurrection—and

1. Teilhard de Chardin, *Divine Milieu*, 117.
2. Whitehead, Griffin, and Sherburne, *Process and Reality*, 343.

it is Christ's. It is all one in him, multiple in us—begun and perfected by him, and yet completed by us."[3] So great is the influence of the oneness, the singularity of deity, that to think in terms of wholeness requires Teilhard to ironically sextuple down on *the one, the one, the one, the one, the one, the one*. McDaniel provides a sample of New Testament backing for the emphasis on extreme monotheism[4] expressed in extreme oneness:

> . . . we are told that Jesus is the "one mediator" between God and humanity (1 Tim 2:5); that there is "no other name" by which persons can be saved (Acts 4:12); that no one comes to God except through Jesus (Jn 14:6); that what took place in Jesus is "once for all" (Heb 9:12) . . . that non-Christians cannot become participants in eternal life, but will depart "into the eternal fire prepared for the devil and his angels" (Mt 25:41), unless before the end of time they become Christian.[5]

Not only is there oneness of God, but also there is oneness of mediation, oneness of savior, oneness of the way to God, oneness of the work of Christ, and oneness of religion. It is peculiar and ironic to observe the proliferation of the varieties of oneness that pervade our thinking. Does this simplification seem like the work of conservative dogmatism? Maybe. But there is a companion liberal failing that also simplifies religious insights into an imperial sameness. For instance, not a semester goes by without a handful of students who wish to write essays about the Golden Rule in every religion. Sure most religions have a version of it, but the implication is that the Golden Rule somehow boils down vastly different religious ways to the lowest common denominator. But, when one truth subsumes all other truths, be wary of an imperial impulse that is busily erasing real, important difference. Simplicity is a tempter. Onlyness is a tempter. Somehow, it seems, the reduction of the vast diversity to the simplicity of *one* implies for us that it must be closer to a basic truth. Meanwhile, reality as we encounter it—Tathata—is nothing if not a sustained lesson in breathtaking diversity, multiplicity, and variety.

Many religious wisdoms have loved the insight of the oneness of God. That view can be wholesome and holy. But the *oneness* of God must not be confused or conflated with God. If the oneness can't be scrutinized, then the elevation of oneness might be a kind of idolatry. Oneness can become

3. Teilhard de Chardin, *Christianity and Evolution*, 73.

4. Monotheism means belief in one (and only one) God.

5. McDaniel, *With Roots and Wings*, 142.

such an idol. When in human minds the oneness itself is mistaken for God, this is evidence of a divine truthiness that can be called the *Cult of Onlyness*. Oneness isn't God. God is God. Oneness is a symbol for how we might talk about God. You might even be convinced it's the best symbol. But, like all symbols, it does not exhaust the genuine truth of what it symbolizes. It does not say all there is to say about God. Divine oneness has limits beyond which the symbol must not be pressed.

When oneness itself is mistakenly regarded as the sacrosanct deity, the Cult of Onlyness results in the proliferation of oneness idols. Elizabeth Johnson's statement that *the symbol of God functions* underscores the danger that the idol of oneness can function to obliterate the many. When the *oneness* of God is the idol it functions by turning God into a monarchical Imperial Ruler.

When people make an error about God, it can lead to tragedies in how we understand human beings—and vice versa. Too often a finite symbol or a finite characteristic is elevated to the status of God, which in turn is enacted by human beings in their sincere effort to conform to divinity. The image-imitation dynamic means, for instance, if people think God is an Imperial Ruler, and then they add to that the belief that humans are created in the image and likeness of *that* God, we can't be surprised to "find" divine authorization for human imperialism. A perverse and self-perpetuating ideology lies at the heart of the Cult of Onlyness: the imperialistic theology empowers imperialistic theological anthropology due to the image-imitation dynamic, which in turn acts as an amplifier and a license to regard imperial humans as supposedly more godlike, superior, more human, better images of God. Worse yet, imperialists then regard non-imperial people as less "godlike," and consequently less human, since they are supposedly less reflective of the image of God, as evidenced by their failure to imitate divine imperialism. (The mind boggles.) Furthermore, the social benefits for perpetrators of imperialism are taken as *evidence* of divine favor to support the imperialist claim that God prefers them. The Cult of Onlyness creates victims, and then uses the fact of victimhood to reiterate the divine approval of its wicked status quo.

What seems to be happening here is that human beings are convinced of the rightness of imperialistic power and are devising notions of divine power to match. When an insidious or vicious element of the world is thought to characterize divinity, the problem is that something finite has been elevated to the status of God. That is the meaning of idolatry, the meaning of divine truthiness: it is junk thought about God.

Leonardo Boff decries this idolatry of the Imperial God, where "God is represented as the absolute Subject who creates subjects so that they may also be creators, like miniature gods."[6] But that means those dehumanized persons are further victimized when people realize that those victims will never be like *miniature gods*. The exclusionary logic of the Cult of Onlyness leaves no room at the top, and does not let in just anyone. Actually, there might be the illusion of inclusion, like the illusion of inclusion in any pyramid scheme, where your cousin needs you to join up or he won't be able to pay the mortgage. But, *why is it satisfactory at all to apply the Cult of Onlyness symbols of emperor, monarch, or king to God?* Historically the most common behavior of earthly emperors amounts to authoritarianism, despotism, and tyranny. The fully functional *Emperor God* symbol is loaded with meaning from our earthly experience of imperialism. The *Emperor God* symbol functions to reinforce truthy notions of a tyrannical God. But what does tyranny have to do with love? Nothing.

How are we to render coherent the absurdity of being required to affirm that God is an emperor (with all we know about tyranny and authoritarianism) while simultaneously holding that "God is love" (1 John 4:8)? The Gospel of John is unambiguous that "God so loved the world that he gave his only Son" (John 3:16) because the God who is love, loves. How does the Imperial God symbol function to build up any notion of the God of love? This is a prime example of the structure of divine truthiness: there is a deep and heartful truth, even a gut truth, admitted in the claim that *God is love*. That gut truth also makes head sense, but divine truthiness mangles divine love by equating it with junk thought like tyranny, empire, and violence.

When people are forced to accept incoherencies, the head and heart are wrenched apart. When the emperor has no clothes we have to be free to say *the emperor has no clothes!* With his usual pith, Charles Hartshorne gives us permission to stop worshipping a tyrant: "Tyrannical people may worship a tyrant God, but why should the rest of us do so?"[7] If we stop worshipping the tyrant God, perhaps we will have less tolerance for the tyrannical behavior of tyrannical people—because we have erased the theological foundation for their tyranny. In his final State of the Union address, President Obama

---

6. Leonardo Boff, *Cry of the Earth, Cry of the Poor*, 197.

7. Hartshorne, *Omnipotence and Other Theological Mistakes*, 59.

quoted Pope Francis on this exact issue: "to imitate the hatred and violence of tyrants and murderers is the best way to take their place."[8]

Martin Luther, in his famous protestations against the abuses of the Christian church of his era, notes the twisting of a wholesome truth about the human stewardship of creation. It was evident to Luther in his reading of the Apostle Paul that followers of Christ should be regarded "as servants of Christ and stewards of the mysteries of God" (1 Cor 4:1). There is nothing inherently wrong with that. But, Luther sees that when the church identifies God as the emperor of the world, and then in turn seeks to emulate that Imperial God, "that stewardship . . . has now been developed into so great a display of power and so terrible a tyranny that no heathen empire or other earthly power can be compared with it."[9] Basically, he determined that their stewardship was not *trustworthy* (1 Cor 4:2), though in stronger terms. Again, a faulty theology (*words about God*) is amplified in human existence by a faulty theological anthropology (*image of God*) and results in abuses and the creation of victims (the *imitation of* an Imperial *God*). So, Luther was dealing head-on with the effects of the image-imitation dynamic when the regime of divine truthiness enforced its view of the Imperial God.

A more contemporary example would be the present-day imperialism called *globalism* or *globalization*. Boff minces no words: "globalization transforms everything in a kind of homogeneous Big Mac."[10] This process of standardization has the effect of erasing authentic diversity and difference. There are seemingly innocuous brands of standardization when "we see the same kind of style for hotels, dress, films, music, and television programs."[11] Yet even these mild examples insidiously delegitimize alternative approaches to ordinary cultural forms (What should a hotel feel like? How should we dress/act? What should we watch/ listen to? etc.) Imperialism erases difference by consuming it, containing it, and removing it by whatever means it chooses. It cannot help itself: empire eradicates difference. When it happens, often in those little ways—when we lose the flavor for homemade chicken and are seduced by fried chicken franchises—we are groomed to accept standardization and homogenization as if it were normal, and so we permit it even in our sacred grounds. The elevation of the worst sort of human imperialism to the level of divinity is divine truthiness

---

8. Obama, "President Obama State of the Union Address 2016."

9. Luther, *On Christian Liberty*, 30.

10. Boff, *Global Civilization*, 51.

11. Ibid.

at work, invading and corrupting everyday existence (even for people who explicitly believe in no God at all).

The deep-seated habit of the Cult of Onlyness—worship of the *one*, the *mono*, instead of worshipping God, the *Theos*—sets the table for each new mono-idolatry. Boff describes the political consequences of a monotheism that is twisted into this Cult of Onlyness: "Monotheism . . . has frequently been invoked to justify authoritarianism and centralized power. The claim has been that just as there is a single God in heaven there must be a single Lord on Earth, a single religious head, a single head keeping order in the family."[12] The all-powerful emperor in the sky, who creates losers and winners, paves the way for earthly emperors, convinced they have a divine right and a blessing to strive to imitate that Imperial God.

Where in this entire description of the Imperial God is anything that approximates genuine love as empathy? Where is the generosity? The gratitude? Where is the upholding of the sacred solitude—the integrity of individuals? Where is the blessing of solidarity—the holy communion among all? In the truthy notion of the Imperial God and the Cult of Onlyness, love is absent. When love is absent, God is absent. The love of God cannot be equated with the creation of victims in a tyrannical ideology, a tyrannical economy, a tyrannical religion. Love can't be tyranny. The problem here is we are being fed a diet of a perverse divine power twisting divine love into despotism. If love as tyranny is the best religions and theologians can muster, we now know better than to believe it. It is divine truthiness, through and through.

12. Boff, *Cry of the Earth, Cry of the Poor*, 79.

Chapter 12

The God Who Doesn't Suffer

The tyranny of the Imperial God takes terrifying shape in the imitation of a God who *could* relieve suffering, but does not. After all, if God is good and all-powerful,[1] yet suffering exists—and it does—then how is such a God justified?[2] This familiar and important protest is not without merit and deserves a coherent response. But Christianity has developed a very complex relationship with the question of suffering—so that makes responding a little harder. In her essay entitled "In Search of Justice: Religious Pluralism from a Feminist Perspective," Marjorie Suchocki observes, "the ill-being of women, blacks, and others outside the dominant cultural value system has been called well-being within a posited system of order."[3] This twisted logic must be called what it is: *evil*.[4] She is right. The divine love cannot be the perpetrator of atrocities. The divine love cannot be the creator of victims.

Divine Perfection and Suffering

A further difficulty is the largely unanalyzed notion that God's perfection *must* mean a divine inability to suffer. The God who cannot suffer is known as the *Impassible God*—a teaching that has undergone major revisions in much progressive theology over the past century, so that now in some circles it is thankfully no longer possible to imagine a God totally detached from creaturely suffering. For instance, in their book *Christian Systematic Theology in a World Context*, Smart and Konstantine see some resolution to

1. Much more on the omnipotence of God in chapter 18.
2. This field of theology is known as *theodicy*.
3. Suchocki, "In Search of Justice, 158.
4. Ibid.

the atheist protest against the good and powerful God who allows suffering. For them, "the so-called problem of evil has to be seen in the context of the doctrine of creation, and in turn this has to be seen in the context of the idea of incarnation . . . Thus a God who undergoes the sufferings of her own creation is different from an aloof impassible Creator."[5] Thus the Christian dogmas of incarnation (God takes on a frail human body that is capable of suffering) and crucifixion (a humiliating and painful kind of execution) are evidence of genius in Christian theology: those teachings mean God is not shielded from suffering.

Only the truthy stoic God enforces so-called love through natural catastrophes, or human violence. Even if this *aloof, Impassible*[6] God has recently been banished in some theological and academic circles, a strong current of agreement about a God who cannot suffer remains popular. The aloof, Impassible God is hard to defend in light of the cross of Christ, which says suffering comes upon God, at least *in some way*. The key to the persistent belief that God cannot suffer is confidence in the idea that perfection has to be static. In contrast, suffering is about changing from one state to another. If someone is convinced that God must be a kind of perfection that cannot change, then the possibility of God suffering seems an illogical leap. Static perfection makes it difficult to apply categories of suffering to God, since suffering implies dynamic change instead of static sameness. People seem to *want* a God of absolute, unchanging perfection that does not suffer. The thought seems to be, if even God is subject to suffering, then there might be no hope for the end of creaturely suffering.

With those sorts of vague thought processes the popular mind continues to elevate a kind of aloof, absolute, unchanging, unaffected perfection as the ideal of divine love. Unfortunately, this suffering-free God delegitimizes the experience of real victims. When God is utterly free of suffering, suffering itself becomes a failure to reflect God. Meanwhile, the imperial rulers, at the top of the hierarchy, whose suffering is reduced by the increase of the suffering of others, are *felt* in some way to be more "godlike." All one has to do, it would appear, is look at the "blessings" of ease and comfort that abound in their lives as "evidence" of divine favor. The problem is deepened by the stance that an all-powerful, perfect God is a God who is in total control—which means that suffering is allowed to exist precisely by the unthwartable

5. Smart and Konstantine, *Christian Systematic Theology in a World Context*, 113.

6. Note: with the alteration of just one letter, the *impassible* God is actually the *impossible* God.

willpower of God. Hemmed in by such theology, God appears to inflict suffering. Therefore people who inflict suffering appear to be *even more* like that truthy God. Calling the worst of human vices "divine" not only absolves the perpetrators of responsibility, it divinizes them and encourages *more* suffering . . . and the cycle continues to spiral onward, outward, out of control.

The final step in this perverse dynamic unfolds when the enforcers of suffering are faced with the horror they have unleashed, and again are bolstered by their fundamental theology: *just as the God who enforces suffering is not required to alleviate that suffering, it stands to reason (in this unfortunate thought process) that neither are the humans who enforce suffering required to alleviate the suffering they unleash.* Perversely, the torturers are convinced they are absolved from their responsibility to assist the people they've crushed.

Without recognizing the rank irony, those who inflict suffering demand that those they have harmed must *pull themselves up by their own bootstraps.* Suffering and oppression take many forms: the withholding of money, rights, access, privilege, education, housing, nutrition, transportation, opportunity, hope, dignity, respect, livelihood, speech, franchise, citizenship, etc. Without irony, Christ's cross is wielded as a weapon against oppressed people when they are told that they must bear their suffering as a "cross"; told they must bear their denied self-actualization[7]; told those sufferings are seen by God, who will redeem them with a blissful life when this life finally ends; told *your life will be great once you're dead.* The perverse promise of otherworldly reward for courageous suffering now has been a major weapon used in the long war waged upon people who suffer at the hands of those in power.

We are right to name this what it is: abuse and evil. But, even Jesus' very own words, "The poor you will always have with you" (Matt 26:11), are used for the cruel purpose of maintaining the lethal status quo. The God who does not suffer, it would seem, is best imitated and best reflected in human beings who suffer least. That is divine truthiness writ large: the worst of humanity is elevated to the status of divinity. The words of Christ are contorted to uphold a status quo that manufactures victimhood. The truthy God is the aloof God who does not suffer. The truthy God is the *perfect monster,* the twisted parent who cannot empathetically love (see chapter 7). A perfectly monstrous, suffering-free God who creates victims is best reflected in the monstrous humanity of those who also create victims.

---

7. According to Abraham Maslow's hierarchy of needs.

The image of God imitates the God who is imagined. But, remember we are looking for the God who is empathetic love—marked by solitude and solidarity (mutuality), generosity and gratitude (reciprocity). The aloof God who does not suffer is the exact *opposite* of divine love, genuine empathetic love, *perfectly inclusive* love. It is so much more wholesome to say that the loving God is our "great companion—the fellow-sufferer who understands."[8] Meanwhile, the God who does not suffer is a terrifying construct of the regime of divine truthiness. So, the God who does not suffer can't really be God.

8. Whitehead, *Process and Reality*, 351.

Chapter 13

The Absolute Moralist God

The issue of divine power is nowhere more evident in religious thought than in conversations about what we are *supposed to do*, how we are *supposed to act*: that is, in questions about morality. Morality that comes from God swiftly becomes an absolute or universal morality, where the closed-circuit logic makes escape seem impossible. The Absolute God who absolutely decrees an absolute morality is hard to evade. The problem is the God who is the Absolute Moralist is really a further elaboration of the Imperial God. Now, because empire is immoral to the core, these impulses toward absolute morality and an Absolute Moralist God are fertile soil for divine truthiness. The divine love in empathy, reciprocity, and mutuality does not align with an immoral Imperial God. It is a mockery of the genuine God of love to call *im*morality the divine will. The consecration of human imperial vices on the altar of divine morality confuses and corrupts the normal religious understanding that God's will defines morality.

The confounding conundrum gets worse when we consider that the whole point of saying a morality comes from God is to require people to live according to that morality. But, if God is the unchanging, perfect, and moral One, then human existence of constant change cannot possibly emulate God's changeless moral goodness. The issue of divine love's morality as the incompatible model for human morality presents a confounding riddle.

The thing is, religious people wish to learn about the nature and desires of God so that they can emphasize in their own lives whatever is more like God, and deemphasize whatever is less like God. Here again is the image-imitation dynamic. But, we are left with moral ruin when we simultaneously try to hold 1) the desire to imitate God, and 2) the notion that God's goodness has nothing to do with us because we can't even approximate it. This becomes a full-blown moral catastrophe when the divine moral codes are imbued with absolute, universal authority. Absolute universal moral codes turn Bronze Age morality into the incontestable, unchanging divine iron will in a much-changed world. But unchanging divine morality is incompatible with the complex reality of a world in the flux of mutual becoming. Only by embracing dynamic divine love in all its complex reality can we be rescued from the incoherent urge to imitate the truthy God who is impossible to imitate.

Now, the most ordinary expressions of divine morality come in the form of moral codes. Of course, the Ten Commandments may be the most famous of them all. Whitehead's book *Modes of Thought* deals a bit with morality, and especially those "codifications" of morality that "carry us beyond our own direct immediate insights."[1] He argues that codifying moral absolutism "only weaken[s] [its] influence by exaggerating [its] status."[2] To illustrate the weakness of absolute moral codes (even ones we are told come from God), he calls to mind the Ten Commandments. He asks, "can we really hold that a rest day once in seven days, as distinct from six or eight days, is an ultimate moral law of the universe?"[3] He is right: authentic morality cannot be ultimately concerned with arbitrary numbers. When pressed to the theological breaking point, where an absolutist line *must* be drawn because of chaotic incoherence, the next problem is we must cast aside our brains *yet again* in order to sustain the unsustainable. First, we are driven to exaggerated moral codes because of incoherent theologies, and second, those exaggerations are a further assault on our intelligence, requiring yet further reliance on dogmatism.

Here is a summary of the moral conundrum for absolute morality composed of incongruous elements: 1) we posit a God who is love; 2) we posit a God whose will is equated with a code of what is good and right and moral; 3) we posit a God who demands that code of morality to be enacted; 4) we posit a human existence so utterly different from God that it is not possible to follow the moral code; and 5) we are hopelessly lost, unable to live a moral life unless we are the recipients of a supernatural intervention. The cost is too great: it is dehumanizing to be forced again and again to marginalize intelligence in favor of an incoherent theology.

Ground zero for this problem of divine truthiness is that divine power overwhelms divine love. Where in a changeless absolute moral code is there room for any empathy for creatures composed of change? The God who is

---

1. Whitehead, *Modes of Thought*, 14.
2. Ibid.
3. Ibid.

cast as the Absolute Moralist starts to appear to be a kind of *demonic* God who demands the impossible from creatures who are categorically incapable of moral living. Being forced to conclude that the love of God is a kind of demon who demands the impossible and punishes those who fail is dehumanizing incoherence. And dehumanizing incoherence is a sure sign of divine truthiness.

Human Morality in a Vast Universe of Expansive Time and Space

Now, if God is the Absolute Moralist who delivers absolute laws for moral beings to absolutely adhere to, there are other problems to confront. What does it mean to say that in the vastness of the universe human moral behavior is God's primary (only?) concern? The implications are manifold. Cobb and Griffin state the difficulty well: "The . . . doctrine, which sees God's primary concern to be the development of moral attitudes, is in the uncomfortable position of maintaining that over 99 percent of the history of our planet was spent in merely preparing the way for beings who are capable of the only kind of experience that really interests God."[4] To elevate absolute morality in this way is a kind of anthropocentric hubris that regards almost everything in the entire universe, for its fourteen-billion-year cosmogenesis, as less important to God than human moral activity. This attitude is in the *uncomfortable position* of maintaining that *almost everything is devoid of the only kind of experience that really interests God.* Are we numb to this because we are so frequently served up heaping helpings of absurd ideas about God?

Status Quo

One final dangerous dynamism in the perilous task of casting God as the Absolute Moralist is that we may wind up divinely enshrining the status quo. Again, I refer to Cobb and Griffin, who express well how this enshrinement comes and how the truthy God becomes the champion of the status quo:

> The notion of God as Cosmic Moralist has suggested that God is primarily interested in order. The notion of God as Unchangeable Absolute has suggested God's establishment of an unchangeable order for the world. And the notion of God as Controlling Power

4. Cobb and Griffin, *Process Theology*, 56.

has suggested that the present order exists because God wills its existence. In that case, to be obedient to God is to preserve the status quo.[5]

Consider: an impossibly tiny fraction of the totality of reality—human moral action—becomes the hinge of meaning for everything. The problem is compounded with the absolutizing of the moral code, which further restricts the already narrow boundaries of meaning. Now add to this situation an unthwartable will of an Imperial God, and we are forced to conclude that whatever happens, happens precisely because it is the will of that Emperor God. The devastating human conclusion is that the moral order in which we find ourselves, with impoverished victims and enriched victimizers, *must* be the moral will of God. There is no alternative. And what kind of hubris must the victims have if they call into question the status quo (by definition, God's will) that crushes them? After all, the mere fact that it exists has to be evidence that it is the will of the Absolutely Moral and Absolutely Powerful God! This idea of God as the Absolute Moralist is an insidious divine truthiness to which we must no longer be forced to assent.

Please do not misunderstand. I have no doubt God has an affectionate concern for every bit of reality throughout the universe. All creatures are intimately drawn toward their best individual and collective potentiality by this God, who perpetually invites, calls, and urges us to build more and more worth, value, and meaning by a loving collaboration with God and the world. And the moral life of human beings is a part of this irreducible worth and value. In fact, it seems that the moral life has the distinct and risky possibility of either intensifying and increasing that worth through moral actions, or of spoiling (to some degree) that worth through immoral actions. So morality is important. But it cannot be the only important thing. There cannot be such an absolute morality as the primary divine concern when it fails to apply to the overwhelming majority of our universe. Furthermore, we should stop endorsing a theology that implies that God requires the status quo, this present order of society. An ideology like that serves to comfort the comfortable and afflict the afflicted, and leads us to the false idol of a demonic and truthy God.

Is it possible to discern genuine divine love in the Absolute Moralist God? Human morality comes alive where the genuine individual meets the community. And the individual and community of human existence are in perpetual change. How can the divine love be genuine empathetic love

5. Ibid., 9.

if it imposes the exact same absolute, universal morality on every person and every community in every circumstance for all time? The emphasis on absolute morality squeezes out divine mercy and divine love. Absolute morality is more like the opposite of empathy, because empathy requires dynamically meeting actual persons and actual communities in the truth of their actually unfolding existence.

Surely, God cannot be the Absolute Moralist who ignores actual conditions. God cannot be the Absolute Moralist who endows the status quo with the divine blessing that crushes the weak and caters to the powerful. When divine power renders divine love meaningless in those ways, we know we have misunderstood divine power. To be forced to believe in the Absolute Moralist God is another dehumanizing and demoralizing defeat at the hands of divine truthiness. But we can rise up from that defeat and denounce the truthy God, and take our place beside the God who is love.

Chapter 14

The Statically Perfect, Unmoved Mover God

The next divine truthiness we must face is the notion of God as the statically perfect Unmoved Mover. Of course we recently encountered the static perfection of the divine inability to suffer.[1] Now, add to static perfection's error the notion of *Unmoved Mover* from Aristotle, which emerges in a matrix of thought that imagines causality as if it were links in a chain, or dominoes arranged one to topple the next, etc. The theology of the statically perfect Unmoved Mover believes there must be a first cause that sets all other causes in motion, but insists the originator of movement is not itself moved by anything else.

It is through the church doctor and scholastic thinker Thomas Aquinas (d. 1274) that this Aristotelian notion of the *Unmoved Mover God* passes fully formed into Christian dogma. As Aquinas says, "God is the First Mover, and is Himself unmoved."[2] Dionysius the Areopagite, a prime articulator of a neo-Platonist Christianity, also influences Aquinas. The term *Unmoved Mover* requires an idea of static changelessness as perfection, and it is certain that Dionysius informs Aquinas's thought with statements like the following on whether we find any change in God:

> And Sameness is attributed to God as a super-essentially eternal and Unchangeable Quality . . . not subject to change, declension, deterioration or variation, but remaining Unalloyed, Immaterial, utterly Simple, Self-Sufficing, Incapable of growth or diminition [*sic*], and without Birth, not in the sense of being as yet unborn or imperfect, nor in the sense of not having received birth from this source or that, nor yet in the sense of utter non-existent; but in the sense of being wholly or utterly Birthless and Eternal and Perfect

1. The interrelation of the various examples of divine truthiness should be no surprise, since everything mutually becomes with everything else. For good or ill, mutual becoming is the Tathata of reality.

2. Thomas Aquinas and Kreeft, *Summa of the Summa*, 75.

in Itself and always the Same, being self-defined in Its Singleness and Sameness, and causing a similar quality of the Identity to shine forth from itself upon all things that are capable of participating therein and yoking different things in harmony together.[3]

The Unmoved Mover is not subject to any change, but is the source of the change in all beings. That is a highly specific idea of perfection as change-lessness—often called *divine immutability*. So, through the great Thomas Aquinas, Plato and Aristotle conspire in the *Summa Theologica* to dogmatize a particular version of static unmoved perfection into the Christian imagination.

Now, perfection as changelessness is not the only opinion available, even though its influence over minds and hearts is so complete that it seems almost impossible to imagine perfection any other way. Happily, we do have options. But, Aquinas warns against falling into the trap of lightly dismissing this kind of static perfection of the Unmoved Mover as the mere buildup of Greek philosophical influence. He points out that in the biblical book of Malachi we find the following words placed in the mouth of God: "For I, the LORD, do not change" (Mal 3:6).[4] Not only in the Bible, but also from Augustine, the highly reliable church doctor, do we learn the same thing, namely, that "God alone is immutable; and whatever things He has made, being from nothing, are mutable."[5] Again we have the doctrine that God does not and cannot change. Aquinas chimes in:

> God is altogether immutable. First, because it was shown above that there is some first being, whom we call God; and that this first being must be pure act, without the admixture of any potentiality, for the reason that, absolutely, potentiality is posterior to act. Now everything which is in any way change, is in some way in potentiality. Hence it was evident that it is impossible for God to be in any way changeable.[6]

---

3. Dionysius the Areopagite, *Dionysius, the Areopagite*, 164.

4. The New American Bible, provided by the US Conference of Catholic Bishops, includes a footnote about this quote from Malachi, indicating that in this case the idea that God does "not change" is said in the context that makes it mean, "God remains faithful to the covenant even when the human partners break it." http://www.usccb.org/bible/malachi/3:1. In other words, God is steadfast in relationship with fickle human beings. That is a far cry from any claim of absolute immutability.

5. Thomas Aquinas and Kreeft, *Summa of the Summa*, 106 (9:2).

6. Ibid., 105., 9:1.

Aquinas believes that whatever is affected by anything else means that it is changed in some way by the interaction. So, he has to plead that God's immutability cannot be affected by anything. In this thinking, change means difference, and when the starting point is unchanging, unchangeable perfection, difference of any kind will always mean less perfection. Less perfection amounts to no perfection. In that framework, it really is all or nothing brinksmanship.

For the notion of an *Unmoved Mover* to make sense, causality must be unidirectional in the manner of links in a chain. Meanwhile, causality in mutuality of becoming envisions *mutual influence in every direction*. But, when linear causality is the guiding principle, we are faced with two options: either the chain of links into the past is never ending—this is called *infinite regress*, which is logically untenable—or there must be a "first cause." This unidirectional chain of causality with a simple first being, who moves others but is not moved by anything else, is the bedrock of static divine perfection.

Devotion to the statically perfect Unmoved Mover God leads to thinking terrible things about the dynamically imperfect moved-ness of literally every other thing besides God. When static perfection is the ideal, "changeless order is conceived as the" real meaning of "perfection, with the result that the historic universe is degraded to a status of partial reality,"[7] or illusion. Many religions have worked themselves into this corner with the sense that this world is illusion—so the concerns of this world, being illusory, are not worth our effort. Only some other supernatural world is worth our energy. Oddly, the idea of a worthless or illusory creation is built on paradox. First, if this world is devalued or understood as mere illusion, then that ignites an intense striving for some *other* world, the supposedly real world, which is the only worthwhile and valuable changeless world. But second—and this emphasizes the confusion—the very stage upon which the striving for that valuable changeless world is to take place is supposedly an illusion: this illusion-world here and now. We are left wondering how striving is possible if the means by which we strive are also illusion.

The situation is confounding. The severe separation of the changelessly perfect God and the depraved changeful world means that if the depravity of change in any way enters God, God may be compromised. These theologies insist that the utter separation between God and the world must be maintained in order to protect divinity from being contaminated by

7. Whitehead, *Modes of Thought*, 80.

illusion, or sin, or imperfection (name your poison). We deserve to be freed from the infection of this divine truthiness that insists that perfection must be static while the actual world of change is unreal, or at least devalued.

We are led to believe God's static perfection is a sacrosanct dogma about God. But is it really? How can it be? There is a beautiful and poetic passage in the *Tao Te Ching* that comes to mind: "a gusty wind cannot last all morning, and a sudden downpour cannot last all day. Who is it that produces these? Heaven and earth. If even the heaven and earth cannot go on forever, much less can man. That is why one follows the way."[8] With words like that, the *Tao Te Ching* encourages sharpness of mind and tenderness of heart to entertain doctrines of divinity that put God into real, relatable relationship with actual creaturely experience. It promotes honesty and freedom to refuse to be cornered into monstrous ideas of God. The words from Lao Tzu's *Tao Te Ching* invite us to consider how change applies to heaven and earth; to consider that something about change itself might have *some*thing to do with the way things really are in their Tathata.

Perhaps the regime of divine truthiness has been too effective at clouding minds for so long that it seems a bit much to wonder if change might in some way apply even to God. Is it a kind of hubris to ask such a question? Actually, the bright philosophical mind of Charles Hartshorne warns the opposite might be true. He wonders if maybe pride is shown in the opposite way:

> To assert that there is no change in any respect or of any kind in God—as it were, to forbid God to change—is to imply: either there is no essentially good kind of change, the lack of which would be a defect, or else God suffers from this defect. Do we know that there is no essentially good kind of change, lack of which would be a defect? I say that we do not know this.[9]

Fascinating. The *real* hubris might be in advocating a concrete dogma that change and becoming cannot apply to God. First of all, when we refuse to imagine that change might in *some* way apply to God, we malign our own existence. Second, and ironically, we belittle the very basis on which we can say that change cannot apply to God. After all, the human mind that arrives at any conclusion is inseparable from the world of change and becoming. The very doctrine against divine change and becoming is *composed* of

---

8. Lao Tzu, *Tao Te Ching*, 28.

9. Hartshorne, *Omnipotence and Other Theological Mistakes*, 31.

change and becoming. So, when we devalue change and becoming as absolutely non-applicable to God because we think they diminish God, we in fact diminish the value of that doctrine because it emerges as a coalescence of components in the world of change and becoming!

Beyond that, it seems that Moltmann agrees with Hartshorne, though he chooses his words more delicately:

> God is not changeable. But that statement is not absolute; it is only a simile. God is not changeable as creatures are changeable. However, the conclusion should not be drawn from this that God is unchangeable in every respect, for this negative definition merely says that God is under no constraint from that which is not of God . . . if God is not passively changeable by other things like other creatures, this does not mean that he is not free to change himself, or even free to allow himself to be changed by others of his own free will.[10]

Divine freedom is at stake, says Moltmann. If we discover that God may in some way change, such a discovery may help us not to fall into broken dualism between static perfection *on high* absolutely contrasted with a dynamic imperfection *here below*. But, will we be so absolutely certain of our dogmatic divine truthiness that we will dare to *forbid God to change*? What if change is not the enemy? What if change and mutual becoming have in their very composition the originating divine love?

Dynamic Perfectioning

In place of that static, unmoved perfection, which leads to monstrous notions of God, it is possible to speak instead about "dynamic perfectioning." Turning the word *perfection* into a gerund hints that static perfection is the illusion, and that if anything resembles *perfection*, it must be a process whereby the richness of dynamic love is understood as *growth*, *maturation*, and *increase* instead of static immutability. *Perfectioning* is a gentle reminder that genuine perfection is not some static lump. Actual perfection is *dynamic perfectioning* that is on the move, on the increase, and on the way.

In order to safeguard the wholesome notion of dynamic perfectioning, it must be recognized that there has been a fourteen-billion-year adventure marked by a kind of *dynamic perfectioning through mutual becoming*. Denis Edwards writes eloquently about how "without the patient unfolding of

10. Moltmann, *Crucified God*, 229.

things in time nothing at all could ever happen."[11] Is it even rational to fear impermanence, fluency, transitoriness, and change when we begin to consider that the very fact that we can consider it at all is a gift with a deep history, since "it takes at least 10 billion years of stellar burning to produce elements like the carbon from which we are made"?[12] If the universe were bereft of impermanence, fluency, transitoriness, and change, the universe would be bereft of us—bereft even of all our theologies, religions, and philosophies.

Edwards says the real source of the fear of change is death. He thinks it is possible to be comforted by the truth that "without death there could not be a series of generations. Without a series of generations there could be no evolution . . . Without death there would be no wings, hands, or brains."[13] But, if that is not sufficient comfort, "Ursula Goodenough writes: 'Death is the price paid to have trees and clams and birds and grasshoppers, and death is the price paid to have human consciousness.'"[14] The massive promise of potentiality comes complete with risks that are just as massive. Risk and promise cannot be removed from one another. The seed of transformation is the urge toward the adventurous possibility of the arising of something really new. But every innovation is only possible because what was achieved earlier has now passed away. The past has had to lose something of its present status. This is the Tathata of our reality of mutuality of becoming. It doesn't have to be the source of fear, since without it nothing at all is possible.

Why should we fear impermanence, transitoriness, and change when genuine love in fact increases in value and intensity with every love communion in every mutual becoming? Even in the midst of horrors and terrors and the inflicting of sufferings, can we in some ways recognize in humanity an achievement of dynamic perfectioning? The greater intensity and value of person-to-person love attraction is made possible when the cosmic process of dynamic perfectioning love expresses itself in the epiphany of *Homo sapiens*. But not only there. Dynamic perfectioning love is the power in every creature to mutually become what it can become.

We should be careful not to think that *dynamic perfectioning* implies that previous beings, like ancestors, are somehow inferior. Our ancestors dynamically participated in the world as it was then. We dynamically

---

11. Edwards, "A Relational and Evolving Universe," 207.

12. Ibid.

13. Ibid., 208.

14. Ibid.

participate in the world as it is now. We would be horribly, tragically, and possibly fatally mismatched to life in the world 150,000 years ago. The persons alive then would be horribly, tragically, and possibly fatally mismatched to life in this world now. Dynamic perfectioning does not mean that we demean the accomplishments of the past. They had a worth and a value that fit that time and that space. And we have a worth and value that fit *this* time and *this* space. And we are indebted to their donations and discoveries.

To refresh the discussion, we can call to mind Hartshorne's observation that in the Aristotelian unmoved mover's "sheer eternity there is no freedom, but in becoming there is some freedom."[15] The fact that ideas about divine immutability might remove freedom from God is cause enough for their dismissal. But we should hold tight to the positive affirmation about the freedom afforded to contingent creatures. It turns out that this same failure pervades much of the ancient world, where change comes not to signify positive freedom, but instead imperfection, brokenness, and suffering. In many ways, this still exists in the popular mind. But this universe of mutual becoming is the only place we can be. If we can't find God here, then we can't find God anywhere.

MuNu

By the enforcement of the divine truthiness of the statically perfect God, we have been thoroughly disintegrated from the most fundamental reality of our lives: the fact of change, impermanence, and mutual becoming (Tathata). Meanwhile, a well-worn and exquisite symbol for God is *Alpha and Omega*. *Alpha and Omega* is a way of symbolically saying God is the beginning and the end of all things by invoking A (Alpha), the first letter of the Greek alphabet, and Ω (Omega), which is the last. Sure, the God of love resides at the beginning and the end. And while it is a lovely and true thought, the fact is we do not live at the beginning or the end. We do not reside at the Alpha or the Omega. We are stuck somewhere in the middle, and we need a symbol for divine love here.

I propose that love is not only Alpha and Omega, but also what we could call *MuNu*—the muddled middle where we experience the ongoing process of dynamic perfectioning. *MuNu* is the combination of the *middle two letters* of the Greek alphabet. MuNu is a symbol for the very heart, the

15. Hartshorne, *Omnipotence and Other Theological Mistakes*, 78.

middle of reality as we encounter it. MuNu implies motion from the MU to the NU. MuNu implies transience in the transformation from one moment to the next. MuNu implies continuity, for in order for the arising of NU, first MU must arise. MuNu implies a real relationship with the beginning, the Alpha, and a real relationship with the end, the Omega. MuNu implies a continuity of interdependence from the Alpha, to the middle MUNU, through to the Omega.

We are creatures in the middle. We are creatures *in-MUNU*, and that is a great gift to be appreciated. To be in-MUNU is not a tragedy inflicted; it is the miracle that makes everything possible. We really don't know that God can't or doesn't change. We don't know for sure that change is really inherently negative. In fact, it seems from our perspective that maybe there is nothing more beneficial to our existence than change. Without impermanence, fluency, and change our mutually becoming existence is over; our life in-MUNU is over.

Not only do we need a more positive notion of impermanence and change in creation—but also in the heart of divinity. After all, the Alpha-and-Omega divinity is the source and goal of in-MUNU existence. Because God is love, the God of Alpha and Omega does not abandon the creatures in-MUNU. Divine love is also in-MUNU (as dynamic perfectioning) in the midst of a changing world. According to Christians the divine love is named Emmanuel (might one even say *E-MUNU-el*?)—which means *God with us*. When we see with eyes of love that appreciate creation as the good gift, the good reflection of divine love, we may be able to take a step into freedom.

Thich Nhat Hanh, the Zen Buddhist teacher, gives an optimistic view of impermanence and in-MUNU existence. His simple wisdom is the wisdom of the Buddha—a wisdom produced by this world. Hanh writes:

> We are often sad and suffer a lot when things change, but change and impermanence have a positive side. Thanks to impermanence, everything is possible. Life itself is possible. If a grain of corn is not impermanent, it can never be transformed into a stalk of corn. If the stalk were not impermanent, it could never provide us the ear of corn we eat. If your daughter is not impermanent, she cannot grow up to become a woman. Then your granddaughter would never manifest. So instead of complaining about impermanence, we should say, "Warm welcome and long live impermanence." We should be happy. [16]

16. Nhat Hanh, *No Death, No Fear*, 41.

While it is often more highlighted in Buddhism, this is a wisdom embedded no less in Christianity. If impermanence is not a teaching of Christianity, what is the meaning of crucifixion and resurrection? Christians say that Christ is divine, so when divinity takes on a human form it is born, it dies, and it is reborn. What in the universe is not like that? *Everything* is like that. If impermanence is not a teaching of Christianity, why does Jesus say in the Gospel of John, "Amen, amen, I say to you, unless a grain of wheat falls to the ground and dies, it remains just a grain of wheat; but if it dies, it produces much fruit" (12:24)? Can the example and teaching of Christ be for the Christian the starting point where it might be possible to admit that God and change are not mutually exclusive? But even more, seeing with eyes of mutual becoming and eyes of love, fosters an understanding that impermanence and change should not be feared. Why would we fear? Impermanence and change describe precisely how divine love dynamically functions *for us*. Since that's the case, there is no need to fear all change and impermanence, because they are the divine gift to creatures in-MUNU.

If frail ordinary creatures can handle impermanence and change, surely God can handle them too. And if your God is threatened by change, we have to ask whether that can really be God. It turns out, the statically perfect Unmoved Mover God is a truthy enigma that turns divine power into a weapon that disfigures divine love. What can love mean for creatures that are always in a process of mutually becoming newness, yet have a God who can do anything except become new?[17] Love without reciprocity, love without mutuality, love without empathy, love without change and growth is a curious riddle because static love, devoid of empathy, is not love at all. It is yet another example of divine truthiness.

---

17. In the summer of 2011, Bruce Epperly's class in Claremont, CA wrestled with this perplexing question of a God who somehow can't do anything new.

Chapter 15

The Supreme Owner God

The statically perfect Unmoved Mover God is divine truthiness through and through—and our recognition of that lays the groundwork for the perverse (though rarely explicit) sense of God the Supreme Owner. Owners get to do what they want with their property—and property doesn't really have much say. If God is an owner, is God the Supreme Owner of the universe? Even though people seldom talk about divine ownership, it is unavoidable to deal with this, because the idea that God really is the ultimate owner of the universe is a largely unanalyzed concept that haunts theology. When Psalm 24 begins by saying, "The earth is the LORD's and all it holds, the world and those who dwell in it," it is hard to avoid the image of God as the owner. It's a disturbing image because of what we know about human owners, and how they often ruin and/or abuse their property. God the Supreme Owner is a symbol that functions. Divine ownership is a symbol of the truthy God because the symbol of ownership inevitably points to so many deadly forces in our world today.

Moltmann makes this symbol of divine ownership explicit in his writing when he observes, "for the modern Western religion of scientific-technological civilization . . . [t]he transcendent God stands over against the world. It is God's property."[1] The ambiguity of the symbol *property*, because of the terrible track record of people being poor caretakers of their property, can lead to devastating consequences. Moltmann nimbly spells out just how that logic concludes. He argues that because of the theological anthropology that claims humans are the image of God, "if God is the Lord of [everything], then humans must become lord of the earth. If God is owner of heaven and earth, then the human must become the owner of

1. Moltmann, "God Is Unselfish Love," 117–18.

77

the nature of the earth."[2] He is describing how God is viewed as the absolute subject in relation to the absolute object—the entire universe.

He warns the second step in this problem is the imitation of the owner God by human beings who are created in the image of the Owner God. If God is the ultimate subject and the universe is a mere object, then human beings (who reflect that God) become the supreme subjects on a totally objectified Earth. We are beleaguered with the impression that only mere objects surround us. Mere objects passively await our misuse, abuse, and domination. When we are convinced that we alone are the subjects who reflect the image of God, and God is the owner who can do whatever "he" wants, then the objects that surround us are mere *things* that we are entitled to use however we desire. This attitude allows us to destroy the Earth. My friend Jill Zasadny describes this dynamism to me like this: *God punishes man. Man punishes woman. Woman punishes child. Child punishes dog.* Every act of turning another being into an object for our abuse or use is a perversion rooted in the truthy idea that God is the supreme subject and the supreme owner of things at his disposal.

The interreligious theologian Aloysius Pieris tracks the source of this extreme objectification back to Christianity, which "liberated its converts from the dread of cosmic forces only to deprive them of their age-old practice of communing with nature."[3] The dynamic at work here is the urge to imitate a false and truthy God. When people yearn to align their lives with God, but they mistake God for the Supreme Owner for whom all else is *mere object*, it is no surprise that they succumb to the urge to imitate God by fashioning themselves as the owners who likewise objectify the world they feel is at their quasi-divine disposal.

The Bible doesn't talk about "objectifying" the world. Instead of saying "objectification," the Bible provides the idea of *dominion*, and directly ties it to the *image of God* theological anthropology in Genesis 1:26–28:

> Then God said: Let us make human beings in our image, after our likeness. Let them have dominion over the fish of the sea, the birds of the air, the tame animals, all the wild animals, and all the creatures that crawl on the earth.
>
> God created mankind in his image;
>
> in the image of God he created them;
>
> male and female he created them.

2. Ibid., 118.

3. Pieris, *Love Meets Wisdom*, 15.

> God blessed them and God said to them: Be fertile and multiply;
> fill the earth and subdue it. Have dominion over the fish of the sea,
> the birds of the air, and all the living things that crawl on the earth.

The danger is it can be such a short step from dominion to domination. The theological-anthropological reasoning in these verses of Genesis, saying that God is the big owner with dominion over everything, seems simple but its effects are numerous and treacherous. The addition of the theological anthropology that humans are created in the image of the Big Owner God must therefore mean they are the little owners with dominion over the rest of things. This seems to add up to human beings who are like little gods who get to dominate other beings. When people worship a truthy Supreme Owner God who is a dominator, and they think they are created in the image of a dominator, it really isn't a shock when people take those verses as divine permission to dominate the world they think they own.

A third step in this domination spiral proceeds from the previous two: little dominators objectify not just the external world of things, but they also treat other human beings as if they are objects at their disposal. This is easy once we are convinced that the human owner is the "best" image of the Divine Owner of creation. In the regime of perverse truthy logic, it stands to reason that those humans who are not owners are less human because they are less the image of God. Then it is easier to treat them like things.

Paulo Freire and other liberation thinkers document rampant dehumanization of impoverished people by ruling classes. That dehumanization includes the insidious and hidden dynamism by which the dehumanizers themselves are dehumanized. Freire says that "dehumanization, which marks not only those whose humanity has been stolen, but also (though in a different way) those who have stolen it, is a *distortion* of the vocation of becoming more fully human."[4] When energy is devoted to enforcing the consequences of our idolatry, we waste resources, we waste other human beings, and we waste ourselves. Because it is an example of how, contrary to reason, people elevate something reprehensible to the status of God, this is divine truthiness.

Elizabeth Johnson also sees idolatry at the heart of the dehumanization of the poor. To her thinking, "In the Latin American situation these [idols] are money, the comfort it brings, and the power necessary to make and keep it."[5] Johnson's evidence for idolatry is that "like all false gods, money and its

---

4. Freire, *Pedagogy of the Oppressed*, 26.
5. Johnson, *Quest for the Living God*, 79.

trappings require the sacrifice of victims."[6] Religious devotion to the money god is an assembly line that manufactures oppressors and victims. But that's not the real God, who is love. It is not God, but humans who demand the sacrifice of victims. To think that God wants sacrifice and victims puts God on the side of the oppressors, which is patently absurd. In this case, the deadening activity of objectification and dehumanization is turned into a so-called divine attribute. Those in the ownership class have created a terrible, self-reinforcing syllogism: a) God is the Supreme Owner; b) humans are created in the image of the Supreme Owner God; and so c) to be truly human means to be an owner, which means those who are not owners are less human, less like God, and therefore can be treated like possessions.

In that gross and deadly spiral, empathetic love is nowhere to be found. God the Supreme Owner is a truthy idol because it turns love into violence by empowering oppressors to create suffering victims. God the Supreme Owner is a truthy idol because it demonstrates the failure of empathy; it lays bare the loveless structures that devastate lives. That cannot be divine love.

---

6. Ibid., 80.

Chapter 16

The Male God

In the long history of societies and religions dominated by men at the expense of women, it's not surprising that the predominant and authoritatively sanctioned symbols of God are almost exclusively male. Of course, reducing God to one gender is ludicrous, and dangerous. Insisting on, or even just assuming, a literally Male God creates the illusion of permanent and substantial categories for men and women.

Serene Jones is a Christian theologian who helps to apply the genius insights of feminism to theological problems. Like other feminist and liberation theologians, Jones questions any thought that there is something essential, universal, or natural, such as some unchanging core substance, to being female or being male. Why does this matter? We must be clear about the sex/gender scheme, which "is a tendency in Western thought to identify sexual difference with both biological/physiological dimensions (sex), and dispositional/psychological and social characteristics (gender)."[1] She also talks about binary differences between male and female, differences that can be interpreted as opposites, complementarity, hierarchy, absence/lack, degrees of difference, or essentialism.[2] Those gender binaries are familiar in idea pairs like male/female, public/private, spirit/matter, straight/curved, and reason/intuition, to name a few. These are cultural constructions that link the first item in the pairs to a narrative of supposedly dominant maleness, while linking the second item in each pair to a narrative of supposedly subordinate femaleness.[3] The over-simplification in each of these examples has a suspiciously truthy character.

Feminist theory requires efforts to *denaturalize* those gender binaries, since when they go unquestioned we live with the illusion that they are a

1. Jones, *Feminist Theory and Christian Theology*, 27.

2. Ibid., 26–27.

3. Ibid., 28.

given, the illusion that historical subordination of women is "natural" and to be expected and not possible to reverse in the present or the future. Without denaturalizing them, they can seem irreversible and incontestable.[4] Feminist constructivism clarifies that, far from being natural, they are merely thought-structuring lenses through which people view the world. The lenses can be changed when we denaturalize the binaries, and recognize that gender characteristics are socially constructed and not a constant given across all cultures.

Jones describes the self in feminist thought as dynamic and composed, rather than stable and simple. The self is the dynamic site of a web of relations, attitudes, causes, and effects,[5] not unlike *jen*, co-humanity, and *ubuntu* (chapter 10, Key Concept 2), or the fact of mutual becoming. For Jones, telling the story of such a self is a matter of metaphorical archeology. By that she means there are many layers to be excavated, and those layers together are "thick." So the description is called just that: thick.[6] This is theology that constructs its thought by relying on whatever happens to be present. What has come together in one dynamic self is analogous to this creative construction, which is the emergent dynamic self of interrelationship. The self is a social construction of causes and conditions, people and experiences, material and ideological realities. A dynamic self composed of relations, composed of the relatedness of mutual becoming, leads Jones to "debunk" the supposedly categorical badness of dependence:

> Once we debunk the notion that dependence is bad, we can discern the various forms that dependency takes and the kinds of power relations that undergird them . . . one can develop models for social cooperation that value the varying degrees to which one person needs another . . . One can also identify structurally coercive forms of dependency . . . in order to minimize their debilitating consequences and to 'denaturalize' the dominant order's account of their origin.[7]

In fact, the basis for every creature is dependency—or better, *mutual dependency*. We don't just become, we *mutually become with all else*. We must analyze healthy dependence and diagnose unhealthy dependence. When we unmask the social construction of dependency structures, we

4. Ibid., 85–90.
5. Ibid., 37.
6. Ibid., 39.
7. Ibid., 85.

might at last see the mechanisms of violence against women, for instance, and begin to understand how to denaturalize them. Such violence is not an inevitable, natural, essential force of nature to which we must simply yield. Yes, we are impacted by pervasive structures of sin (think *original sin*, perhaps)—but they are not the whole story.

What we find in Jones is a powerful expression of the greatness of feminist thought: *interrelational mutuality*. In like fashion, Elizabeth Johnson talks about how "feminist theologies embrace [this] alternative vision of community, one of equality and mutuality between sexes, races, classes, all peoples, and between human beings and the earth, and actively seek to bring this vision into reality."[8] But, the shadow side of mutuality is also true: there is a web of interlocking oppressions, with many faces (racism, sexism, militarism, colonialism, etc.). One side requires the other; the removal of one is the removal of the other. Potential and risk rise and fall together in a world of mutual becoming.

Distorting God, Women, Men, Love

The emphasis on mutuality and reciprocity as the basis for understanding relations, and love brings into sharp focus a long-standing distortion of love by truthy theism. When the divine love can only be understood as active and outward without any sense of receiving back anything from the beloved, love loses its essential characteristics of compassion and empathy. In other words, reciprocality is missing. But what is love without reciprocal mutuality of empathy? That would mean love is not actually love—and that is a massive red flag. One-sided and unidirectional love is a highly gendered and truthy idea.

Massive consequences accumulate when the binaries of men and women are absolutized, universalized, and naturalized, to the point where simple observations about the physical workings of sexual relations between men and women are elevated to the status of God. Make no mistake: it is coarse and offensive. To say God's love is unidirectional is a false and truthy characterization of divine love. In the traditions that idolize God's maleness, this supposedly unidirectional divine love is perversely aligned with a highly gendered notion of male-instigated heterosexual intercourse: God's love is said to *go out into* creation, to *penetrate* creation, and even to *seed* creation (i.e., *logos spermatikos*). In that construction, truthy divine

8. Johnson, *Quest for the Living God*, 94.

love is outgoing, and the creation is nothing but the passive receptacle. The genderizing continues as the sexual receptivity of the woman is perversely equated with a lesser love, while the sexual outgoing of the man is aligned with that supposedly outgoing-only divine love.

The truthy Male God does not receive. In fact, he can't receive. This peculiarly male truthy God's love *only* gives. Joan Wingert points out to me how even though "this giving sounds generous, the going out, the penetration and the seeding may or may not be invited or welcomed. If the world is truly passive, the receiver *must* take what is given without choice or voice." It is exactly here that the truthy construct of a literally Male God is exposed. Genuine love with mutuality and reciprocity known as empathy does not bulldoze the beloved.

The elevation of active giving love as the only kind of divine love, with the accompanying diminishment of receptive love, eliminates all possibility of divine love as reciprocal mutuality. According to the regime of divine truthiness, when the maleness of God is idolized, the male human is found to therefore be more reflective of divinity, and the female human suffers what appears to be a perversely justifiable oppression at the hands of men. It is a vicious spiral that leaves us with a twisted notion of one-sided and unidirectional love that can't really be love, because empathetic love can never be unidirectional.

Real love is not unilateralism. But, under the strain of divine truthiness, religion has so thoroughly idolized the maleness of God that we are shackled, it seems, to a perverse kind of divine love that is incapable of receiving anything back from the beloved. We might say it is an impermeable or an impregnable kind of love. We are presented with a truthy divine love aligned with an allegedly impregnable maleness as opposed to allegedly pregnable femaleness. The truth is, neither of these is correct: there are aspects of maleness that can be and are impregnated, and there are aspects of femaleness that are impregnable. Neither characteristic resides in only one gender. But the gross contours of the literally-male-God paradigm reduce God and humanity to dangerous oversimplifications.

The Impenetrably Impermeable Male God

The God who is known by the male terms *Father* and *Son* and the gender-nonspecific—at least in English,[9] that is—term *Spirit* inclines the mind to-

9. In Hebrew, the word for *spirit* is a feminine noun, *ruah*. In Greek, *spirit* is the neuter

ward androcentric (male-centered) notions of God, and toward supposed divine permission for patriarchy.[10] Patriarchy is not a neutral phenomenon, not a mere inconsequential flip of the gender coin. Neither is it a *natural* phenomenon. Whitehead laments the effects of patriarchy, and notes how they are intensified, rather than diminished, in civilization: "A rule of men over women remained an established feature of highly civilized societies. It survived as a hang-over from barbarism. But its demoralizing effects increased with civilization . . . [that] issued in the degradation of women below the level of males."[11] As already indicated, there is something crass and offensive about the observation that the inequality *seems to be based on sexual and physical attributes*. And we *should* be offended—not that Whitehead has made that statement, but offended at the fact that what he says is embarrassingly true. It *is* offensive. Its perpetuation is even more offensive.

The crass and odious theologies that propose an impermeable and literally Male God are the truthy theologies being dismissed here: the tyrannical Emperor God, the Absolute Moralist God, the statically perfect Unmoved Mover God . . . they are each truthy images of a literally Male God. When taken together, those so-called divine attributes amount to one comprehensive category: the literally Male God who cannot be permeated in any way. The traditional categories are like bulwarks set up to prevent God from being permeated by any created thing; to prevent God from being infected by change in any form; to ensure God is impregnable.

The resulting false image of divine love cannot really be love because empathy requires the ability to receive the other into the self in some way. How can we call it love when empathy's reciprocity, a necessary requirement of love, is absent from that literally Male God? The Christian tradition pleads that, in the peculiar and solitary case of the incarnation, God *is* permeated by a world of suffering. In Christ, God receives into himself the sufferings of the world. But, even there the case is argued in favor of God's literal maleness because Jesus was sent to Earth in the form of a man.

Notions of an impermeable Male God found their way into the Christian theology of the early centuries in a number of ways. For instance, it is worthwhile to take a moment to read through the armor imagery in the Letter to the Ephesians, which instructs the Christian to

---

pnévma. These linguistic inclinations are lost to English speakers and readers. Meanwhile, for the same audience, the maleness of the symbols Father and Son is beyond doubt.

10. Rule by men.

11. Whitehead, *Adventures of Ideas*, 83.

. . . put on the armor of God, that you may be able to resist on the evil day and, having done everything, to hold your ground. So stand fast with your loins girded in truth, clothed with righteousness as a breastplate, and your feet shod in readiness for the gospel of peace. In all circumstances, hold faith as a shield, to quench all (the) flaming arrows of the evil one. And take the helmet of salvation and the sword of the Spirit, which is the word of God. With all prayer and supplication, pray at every opportunity in the Spirit. To that end, be watchful with all perseverance and supplication for all the holy ones and also for me, that speech may be given me to open my mouth, to make known with boldness the mystery of the gospel for which I am an ambassador in chains, so that I may have the courage to speak as I must. (6:13–20)

That language presents an ideal where Christians must, like God, be impermeable to evil influences. What it's possible to miss is that the only *opening* in such armor is not for something to enter, but rather for something to leave. The Christian exerts the gospel in order that it may penetrate and permeate others. That language mirrors the outgoing-only love of the literally Male God. The unidirectionalism of God's action is mirrored in the Ephesians vision of the role of the Christian, to reflect the supposed impenetrable, literal maleness of God.

According to Peter Brown, in his important book *The Body and Society: Men, Women, and Renunciation in Early Christianity*, impermeable maleness hijacks the heart and mind of Cyprian (bishop of Carthage from 248 to 258).[12] For Cyprian, "the body of the Christian emerged as a microcosm of the threatened state of the Church,"[13] which meant it was potentially vulnerable to invasion and mutilation by outside forces. Cyprian is terrified that the church will be vulnerable as a passive receiver. In *De Zelo et Livore*, Cyprian calls any such vulnerability the "effeminate weakening of the hard resolve of the Christian."[14] The blatant and offensive genderized images are stark and unambiguous.

To be clear, Cyprian actually thinks there is a danger in the sexual permeability of femaleness, to the point that female members of the Christian Church are a *bona fide* threat. And not even a man should dare exhibit so-called female attributes, since that would also be an *effeminate weakening of the hard resolve*. We read further in Cyprian that the devil "goes about every

12. Brown, *Body and Society*, 192.
13. Ibid., 195.
14. Ibid.

one of us; and even as an enemy besieging those who are shut up (in a city), he examines the walls, and tries whether there is any part of the walls less firm and less trustworthy, by entrance through which he may penetrate to the inside," and further, that "he presents to the eyes seductive forms and easy pleasures, that he may destroy chastity by the sight. He tempts the ears with harmonious music, that by the hearing of sweet sounds he may relax and enervate Christian vigour."[15] Reading those passages, it is easy to understand how Brown can describe "a physicality in the writings of Cyprian that crackles with the sense of the flesh as a charged boundary, under constant threat of violation."[16] The *effeminate*, whether in the form of a man[17] or a woman, is a peculiar and dangerous "opening" into which threats may penetrate the *walls* or the *armor* of the Christian or the Christian community. Maintaining impenetrable impermeability means maintaining a male-God-like quality for the Church and for each individual Christian. Cyprian thus becomes a great proponent of perpetual virgins in the church: consecrated, inviolate women who help shore up the walls of Christianity by demonstrating a graceful impermeability.

It is not only in the New Testament Epistles and Cyprian that this sensibility is found. When the church, known as the Body of Christ, is the representative of the Male God, it must maintain rigid impenetrability. More than that, its main duty is to *permeate*—or even, more graphically, to *penetrate*—the rest of the world with its presence, with the gospel, with the will of God, and with the decrees of the church. Truly, in one form or another, this specter hovers over the Christian centuries, and is fed by the fearful and defensive mentality of the canonical Gospels themselves, which were written in the face of the emerging church's potential annihilation by the Roman Empire. We see this even today in pronouncements by televangelists in the United States who, in spite of the large majority of Americans identifying as Christian, proclaim that American Christianity is under some kind of siege. That siege mentality is deep in the scriptural DNA of Christianity, and is likely at the heart of the aversion to openness to outside influences.

What is being described here is Christianity's self-stunting inability to access and express and enact something so true about the cosmic Tathata:

15. Cyprian of Carthage, Treatise 10: *On Jealousy and Envy*, no. 2.

16. Brown, *Body and Society*, 194.

17. We are not wrong to observe here the rudiments of a theology that is opposed to male homosexuality as well, since that sexual orientation seems to imply the importation of a supposedly female permeability into the male.

the ubiquitous fact of mutual becoming, the fact of the universal mutual permeability of everything. Instead, we have too long focused on *God as the active penetrator*. When God is the literally male, active organ of divinity that goes out into a world and seeds it with truth, this should be regarded as a reckless and offensive reduction of the male to a banal physical and sexual attribute. This idolatrously and literally Male God is not receptive, is not permeated, and is not penetrated in any way. This idolatrously and literally Male God is only outgoing. Empathy's reciprocity is non-existent. And that spells trouble for love.

The blindness caused by the idolatrous emphasis on the *maleness of God* and the accompanying devaluing of the femaleness of God results in a dangerous hierarchy in human relations. The idolatrous hierarchy is damaging at every turn: it exalts men as allegedly a truer reflection of God, while it simultaneously degrades women as allegedly less reliable images of God.

The Functioning of the Male Symbol for God

The foregoing examples reignite the truth of Elizabeth Johnson's astute maxim: *the symbol of God functions*. In fact, the male symbol of God "is never neutral in its effects, but expresses and molds a community's bedrock convictions and actions."[18] The male symbol of God takes on the lamentable character of being a literal statement about divinity. It becomes a concrete dogma where no such certainty is honestly possible.

The negative reaction from so many folks when female symbolism replaces male symbolism is clear evidence that the male symbol of God functions as a literal idol. If male terms were really only being used as neutral placeholders, with no idolatrous attachments, those replacements would not be met with fury. Too often, the revolt against changing divine gender pronouns is frightening. Johnson points to how this literalization has real effects on real experience, by highlighting how "male images have functioned to justify patriarchy in church and society," and she employs "Mary Daly's inimitable phrase [which] captures the rationale: 'if God is male, then the male is God.'"[19] And exclusive male symbolism of God gives "rise to the unwarranted idea that maleness has more in common with divinity than femaleness."[20] In this way, "exclusively male images imply

18. Johnson, *Quest for the Living God*, 98.
19. Ibid., 99.
20. Ibid.

that women are somehow less like unto God."[21] Johnson correctly points out an implicit and scandalous divine permission for the oppression and dehumanization of more than half of humankind. In chapter 15, it was the poor and non-owners who were thought to insufficiently reflect the image of the Supreme Owner God. Here it is women and girls, who supposedly insufficiently reflect the image of the Male God.

Here the idolatry of the maleness of God results in a long-standing second-class status for female persons, who can never erase the existence of their two X chromosomes. Why should they want to? While the hope in other social reform movements is that there will be success in changing the status of oppressed persons by their emerging as subjects of their own history, and by the alleviation of their misery, in the case of the fact of the existence of women and girls, no parallel reform can be implemented that would change them from being female. The exclusively male symbol of God functions to cast women and girls as less in the image of God, with permanent second-class status. The consequences of the literally Male God are intolerable, though many of us tolerate them routinely. The negative ramifications are immense, but we don't have to keep tolerating them. Can we at last dispense with the divine truthiness called the literally Male God? The hope here resides in the tearing down of the idolatry of the male symbol of God, so that socioreligious structures that are reinforced by that idolatry can be finally dismantled.

Time after time, the destructive element that ruins divine love is a faulty idea about divine power. Time and again, we are peering into the outcomes of our theological thought structures. To clearly see the unwholesome outcomes of these dogmas empowers us to change them. The evidence is in. The verdict is clear: the literal maleness of God is guilty of destroying the lives of women and girls—*and* men and boys—for millennia. We can no longer entertain the protest that the *intent* of the Male God image is good, just so we can ignore its real consequences. When a wrong notion of power turns the divine and human love into a kind of hate—and it is *hate, not love,* that demeans and destroys people—it is long past time to recognize that it is a false idol, and name it for the divine truthiness it is.

21. Ibid.

Chapter 17

Literal Interpretation of the Bible

T he next so-called theological truth (which is in fact just one more divine truthiness) for us to confront is the supposed imperative to engage in a literal reading of the Bible. This is a little different than our others since it is not a wrong stance on God, per se. Here, the method of reading the Bible is the means by which divine truthiness can either be upheld or opposed. Literal reading of the Bible means taking the text as word-for-word absolutely true and factual, without error in any sense. An absolute insistence on a literal reading of the Bible in every case is the sort of divine truthiness that preys on the wholesome, heartfelt desire to take the Bible very seriously. Somehow, a literal reading of the Bible *feels* like it accomplishes that seriousness. But to fully engage one's intellect with literalism exposes a truthy separation of head and heart. But, let's not be extremists in the opposite direction. Let's be honest instead. Let's be open to the possibility that we *might* find some things in the Bible that have profound meaning in *some* literal sense, so we can also be open to the possibility that we will find others that do not.

It is not difficult to see that the exclusively male interpretation of God is linked to a literal reading of the Bible. Mainly, in the Christian theological tradition, the idolatrous maleness of God stems from a literalization of the maleness embedded in *Father* and *Son* as symbols for God. The male Father and male Son symbols for God function by forming imaginations. Then thought structures form society. Then society forms our thought structures . . . That is how a symbol *functions* in a process of self-perpetuating augmentation.

To gauge what a so-called conservative reading of the Bible would be these days, we might think that we are *required* to blindly accept a literal reading. In the United States the predominance of the literalist approach to reading the Bible wrongly implies that literalism is the only faithful approach.

The rampant authority of literalism even seems to imply that literalism is supported by the two-thousand-year history of Christian thought. It's not.

To the best of our ability, we must be diligent in our commitment to a holistic understanding of reality. The holistic approach is the wholesome approach, the holy way—the way that ends divine truthiness. And that means staying committed to heartfulness and mindfulness both, amidst the effort to uproot the insidious falsehoods that have so long been portrayed as unquestionable truth. Peter Gomes shares that commitment. He has written a helpful book cleverly entitled *The Good Book: Reading the Bible with Mind and Heart.* The title evokes our discussion about the mind/heart divide described by Colbert's term *truthiness,* or the divide in theology and religion called *divine truthiness.* His book deals directly with the menacing problem of literalism.

Gomes exposes an inherent falsehood embedded in literalist ideology, namely, that when one reads the Bible literally, it is supposed that one avoids the pitfalls of interpretation. Nothing can be further from the truth because every act of reading *is* an act of interpretation. With a gentle touch, he observes that "there are many devout and sincere Christians for whom the notion of interpretation in scripture is anathema. They argue that scripture has a clear and plain meaning . . . Interpretation is either to add or to subtract from what is already there; it amounts to a form of vandalism . . ."[1] This perspective usually comes complete with a kind of absolutism, a kind of ultimatum-ism: the Bible says what it means, and what it says must either be *all true or all false*! That kind of brinksmanship plays fast and loose with the deeply important and deeply personal issue of the foundations of faith. One must surely be certain of one's certitude to be willing to make such a statement. But, if real life teaches anything, it is that people are fallible, and human ideas are disconcertingly subject to revision in the face of new evidence.

When discussing about the Bible, faith is no small matter. There is something pure and beautiful beneath the intention of the faith statement that the Bible should be read literally. Most literalist readers faithfully acknowledge that God reveals God's loving and powerful self in the carefully chosen words of the Bible. But, God revealing Godself is only part of the equation. To be a literalist means admitting a few things. The first two might not be that controversial: 1) a doctrine that says God is infallible; 2) the sincere best efforts of human beings to write in the Bible their experiences with God. At this point things get dicey when we get to number 3: to be a

---

1. Gomes, *Good Book*, 31.

literalist also requires the reader to infallibly read the text. Surely, we must have enough self-honesty to admit that we are not infallible. Commitment to honesty means it won't be possible to deal in absolutes like literalism.

Even when people can admit they are not infallible, that they are not God, problems with literal readings of the Bible go deeper. For instance, what happens when we find traces of the truthy God even in the Bible itself? An example is this passage in the book of Joshua where God suppposedly orders genocidal extermination of the inhabitants of fallen Jericho, and Joshua obeys "by putting to the sword all living creatures in the city: men and women, young and old, as well as oxen, sheep and donkeys" (6:21). In response to that kind of biblical statement, Bishop Spong, who has a far sharper tongue and pen than Peter Gomes, has said, "I could not believe that anyone who had read [the Bible] would be so foolish as to proclaim the Bible in every literal word was the divinely inspired, inerrant word of God. Yet the claim . . . continues to this day." He then asks, wryly, "Have these people simply not read the text?"[2] By now, reading something like that from the book of Joshua should sound the alarm about a truthy and false divinization of the worst human behavior. How is the genocidal God not evidence of divine truthiness in the Bible itself? The problems of a literal reading leave a person with the clear and horrible sense that God somehow endorses, even *requires*, genocidal extermination of certain human beings.

Because God's love cannot be the commander of genocidal extermination, it seems more wholesome and healthier to endorse Peter Gomes's identification of the "dangers of interpretation" that "take three forms, all related and equally dangerous. These temptations are a form of idolatry."[3] While his previously gentle touch coarsens in this case, he has to be frank here because he sees these three dangerous temptations as the perpetrators of genuine violence. The three idolatries commit violence against sincere believers. Those three idolatries are 1) *bibliolatry*, worshipping the Bible; 2) *literalism*, worshipping the verbatim text of the Bible, often in a particular translation which is arbitrarily chosen as somehow the exclusivly correct one; and 3) *culturism*, worshipping the culture of biblical times, or the culture in which the Bible is being currently read.[4]

Much in the same way as God's maleness has been turned into an idol, bibliolatry, literalism, and culturism function as God-replacement

2. Spong, *Rescuing the Bible from Fundamentalism*, 20.

3. Gomes, *Good Book*, 35.

4. Ibid., 36–51.

strategies dripping in divine truthiness. But, with all these idolatrous dynamics, they can be difficult to discern precisely because the people committing these infractions are often our most religious neighbors and friends. Gomes shares a pithy though unattributable aphorism that warns of the more insidious danger of too much virtue rather than the danger of too much vice: "'A surplus of virtue,' it says, 'is more dangerous than a surplus of vice.' 'Why?' we naturally ask. 'Because a surplus of virtue is not subject to the constraints of conscience.'"[5] Absolute certainty extinguishes further exploration: why go in search of what is already found?

Incurably Vague Dogmatic Certainty

The problem with certainty-laden literalisms and idolatries is that they endow limited and flawed human readings with an ultimacy that should belong to God alone. But, this doesn't only happen in religions. Whitehead calls into question not only our extreme certainties, but also even our more ordinary ones, because of what he calls the *incurable vagueness* in our observational powers. Think for a moment about how everything we know is so very, very fragmented—or *incurably vague*.[6] The scope of human awareness, to be honest, is really sort of tiny, highly localized, and prone to mistakes. But, he does not highlight that incurable vagueness of awareness in order to make us lose hope. He questions dogmatic tendencies so we can replace dogmatic certainty with an attitude of radical self-honesty. People should be honest about limitations. The perverse habit of turning the Bible into a *God-replacement strategy* is a false security that inhibits growth and cheapens hearts and minds.

Once those hearts and minds are freed from literalism, it becomes possible to expose even the Bible to the light of reason, and find where incoherent divine truthiness has infiltrated the texts, find where the divine love is mangled into a kind of hate, and set aside the problem texts. Freed from the truthy junk thought that muses about a supposedly infallible reading of Scripture, we can extend that honesty to the Bible itself. In that freedom, we can call foul when a text seems to imply that divine love approves of and permits slavery, or seems to imply that divine love thinks women are less worthy than men, or seems to imply that divine love enforces itself as war that kills every enemy.

5. Ibid., 51.
6. Whitehead, *Adventures of Ideas*, 145.

Chapter 18

The Omnipotent God

We can declare our freedom from the authoritarian imposition of dogmatic and literalist certainties of divine truthiness. That freedom comes from self-honesty whenever we refuse to elevate humans to the heights of divine infallibility. We ignite this freedom by engaging our whole persons: heart and mind. However, yet another divine truthiness that we are supposed to accept without question threatens our fledgling freedom. It is time to turn attention to the truthy idea that reinforces the other examples of divine truthiness. It is time to dispense at last with what might be the most stubborn divine truthiness: the Omnipotent God.

Omnipotent means *all-powerful*. Omnipotence is a philosophical category for God that means God is all-powerful. Sometimes people say God is *almighty*, and they are talking about omnipotence. The Almighty God is the Omnipotent God, the God who has all the power. Maybe it even seems like an unnecessary statement to say God is omnipotent, because it almost feels like it is a term synonymous with God. In fact, people often refer to God simply as *the Almighty*.

Ordinarily, divine omnipotence seems to be beyond question. Because of that, people fail to question the outrageous implications of divine omnipotence. Does it really mean God has all the power? Does it mean God does not share power? Does it mean God, who has all the power, cannot be contradicted by creatures, who really have no power? If God has all the power and cannot be contradicted, then does that mean everything that happens is what God wants to happen? If everything that happens is what God wants, then does that mean God wants a child to be abused, wishes stage 4 cancer on your beloved, plans the bombing of a daycare . . . ? The questions that don't get asked can be endless.

Every oppressive, deplorable, or intolerable condition is the will of the God with all the power, whose will is inevitably enacted by every powerless

94

creature. Maybe this is why people don't wonder out loud about the consequences of divine omnipotence: when God has all the power, the current state of things, or the status quo, is by definition exactly what God wills it to be (chapter 13).

Perhaps the reader will wish to declare that human free will is a gift from God, and it is through our free will that human beings have brought ruin and destruction to this world. Many people do try to hold up divine omnipotence alongside human free will. But, invariably it is those same people who name each catastrophe, each tragedy, as "God's plan." The reign of omnipotence is hard to crack.

Now, if God really does hold all the power, and the status quo is perpetually troubling (and it is: there has never been a time in history without oppression, war, starvation, deprivation, senseless death, meaningless suffering), then who is to blame? The God who has all the power would seem to be to blame for all of that. Yet, religions are fond of holding *people* accountable, whether by reward or punishment, for their behavior. But, how can that be? If whatever happens is by definition what God wants to happen, (after all, the Almighty's the one with all the power, right?) then how can there be any responsibility, accountability, or meaning in creaturely existence? If it is all an elaborate puppet show, where God is the puppeteer and we are the puppets, it seems somehow less than fair or loving to imagine we might be rewarded or punished for what we do. If God really does have all the power, then nothing else really has a say in what happens, and it would seem the only kind of power that God exerts is the power of total control. It's a confoundingly closed circuit.

So, there seem to be cracks in the supposedly unquestionable edifice of the Omnipotent God. Further difficulties with the notion of the Omnipotent God are the facts that *God is love*, and that *God loves the world*. Since love is empathy that ensures the mutual integrity of individuals in communion of solidarity, and since love works through a reciprocal flow of giving and receiving, then omnipotence isn't even compatible with love. It is especially difficult to explain the horrors inflicted on powerless creatures if they are in fact the will of a supposedly loving Omnipotent God. If the word *love* actually means love, a God who acts like that can't also be symbolized by love. Love does not inflict suffering on powerless creatures.

In his essay "Teleology Without Teleology: Purpose through Emergent Complexity," Paul Davies asks important questions about what we mean by a "powerful"—even an *all*-powerful—God and Father. He asks, which is the greater, more flexible, more generous, and more powerful love: the one that makes all the decisions for the other, or the one that participates in the unfolding experience, offering new options?[1] As he considers the fact of ongoing creation, Davies muses about "how much easier it would be for an omnipotent deity to 'cobble together' the complex systems 'along the way' by crude manipulative intervention . . . but how much less impressive!"[2] What if that statement could sink in? It surely must be a more impressive sort of power that has the flexibility and ingenuity to admit authentic freedom that shares power instead of exerting total control.

If the Omnipotent God exercises coercive power, then where in creation is the room for authentic learning, real growth, and genuine experience? If God can and does coercively intervene, then what happens to responsibility? Meaning? Freedom? They are cast aside. How much more breathtakingly sublime is the thought that God lovingly and generously allows creation to become what it shall become? Davies goes on:

> To select a set of laws that through their subtle interplay bring about a *natural* creativity of an orderly and organizational form, a spontaneous self-organizing potency that is not anarchic but hierarchical and constructive, which is both ordered yet open, determinate in its general trend yet undecided in the specifics, is altogether more wonderful and a cause for celebration![3]

That view *is* cause for celebration. Reflecting on my own life, I can't help but call to mind the rigid authoritarianism of my violently abusive dad. On vacations there was an overwhelming sense of the imperative to *have a good time at all costs*. In spite of the miseries that are an inevitable part of driving cross-country, and the numerous ways we were at the whims of the weather, and allergies, and bladders, and fatigue, it was required by the higher authority of my dad that we enjoy ourselves. On the one hand, it seems an innocuous and benevolent intent, since it would be bizarre to take his family on vacation with the aim that we should all be miserable. But, when our emotional enjoyment was *enforced* by strength of intimidation, and threat of punishment, no one should be surprised at the outcome: it was often with dread that we anticipated these times together. It turns out

---

1. After all, the people I know who enforce their will on others are the worst sort of bullies.

2. Davies, "Teleology without Teleology," 105.

3. Ibid.

that there is nothing so weak, nothing so utterly impotent, as the enforcing of one's will upon another.

Yet, here we are with a sometimes strong, sometimes vague sense that God, *if God is really God*, must have the kind of power to enforce the divine will to overturn natural laws—those ordinary laws that God invented. David Ray Griffin places the center of gravity for omnipotence theology in the everyday assertion that "God created our universe *ex nihilo*, with the *nihilo* understood to mean absolute nothingness."[4] Oddly, the doctrine that God created the universe *ex nihilo*, that is, *out of absolute nothing*, isn't even very biblical. Here, with my own emphasis added, are a few English translations of the first two verses of the Bible, which are supposedly the source for the *creatio ex nihilo* idea:

> In the beginning, when God created the heavens and the earth and *the earth was without form or shape*, with darkness over *the abyss* and a mighty wind sweeping over *the waters* . . . (NAB; emphasis mine)

> In the beginning when God created the heavens and the earth, *the earth was a formless void* and darkness covered *the face of the deep*, while a wind from God swept over *the face of the waters*. (NRSV; emphasis mine)

> In the beginning God created the heavens and the earth. Now *the earth was formless and empty*, darkness was over *the surface of the deep*, and the Spirit of God was hovering over *the waters*. (NIV; emphasis mine)

No matter the translation, these famous verses in Genesis (1:1–2) that portray the beginnings of creation describe something quite different than creation out of absolute nothingness. It is a stunning display of mental gymnastics to imagine that the phrases

> *the earth was without form or shape,*
> *the abyss*
> *the waters*
> *the earth was a formless void*
> *the face of the deep*
> *the face of the waters*
> *the earth was formless and empty,*

4. Ibid., 37.

the surface of the deep
the waters

can somehow be taken to mean *absolute nothingness*. But, Griffin points out, this doctrine of *creatio ex nihilo* took on exaggerated importance in the early disputes between Christian orthodoxy and its Gnostic challengers. The heresy of Marcion "said that our world was created out of evil matter. The best way to fight this idea, they thought, was to deny that the world was created out of anything."[5] But, doesn't it actually seem that a God who faces no resistance whatsoever, and creates in that way, paradoxically demonstrates the most embarrassing kind of powerlessness? A God who creates out of absolute nothing is a God whose efforts are met with no opposition whatsoever, and so such an act of creation requires what amounts to *almost no power: it requires only the tiniest amount of power to overcome no power*.

Christians and Jews should be grateful that what Genesis actually describes is something far more impressive: creation as *collaboration from the start, relation from the start*. There is a tender relationality in those first verses of the Bible. God, for instance, is depicted as enlisting the help of the Earth in creating animals: "Then God said, 'Let the earth bring forth all kinds of living creatures: cattle, creeping things, and wild animals of all kinds.' And so it happened: God made all kinds of wild animals, all kinds of cattle, and all kinds of creeping things of the earth. God saw how good it was." And then as enlisting the participation of the rest of the world in the making of human beings: "Then God said: 'Let us make man in our image, after our likeness'" (Gen 1:24–26). It seems to be the simplest explanation of the plural pronouns ("let *us* . . . in *our* . . . after *our*") that God intends to create human persons collaboratively with the shared work of the previous world full of creations.[6] That is not God the enforcer. That is God the inviter—a God who invites new relations to emerge in a world of mutual becoming.

The collaborative God who invites humans, and every creature, into the act of co-creation animates the saying, "If you pray for potatoes, you'd better have a hoe in your hands." Do we really want magic? Do we really want a God who wiggles her nose and makes potatoes appear? Do we think God intervenes as some kind of coercive overlord genie who upends the laws of nature and fails to let potatoes be potatoes? Who would want a God like that? How much more loving is the God who *shares* power, who lets

5. Ibid., 37–38.

6. Recall Moltmann's idea of theological anthropology that proposes humans are created *both* in the image of God *and* in the image of the world (chapter 10, Key Concept 2).

potatoes be potatoes, and lets people be people; a God who *invites, but does not require* our participation in the cultivation of potatoes!

The deity whose creativity amounts to nothing but coercive enforcement over the powerless is the opposite of a relational and collaborative (loving) God. That's not divine omnipotence. That's more like impotence. This critique against the Omnipotent God brings into focus a more loving, more generous, more powerful God who shares love, generosity, and power with the world.

Suspiciously Truthy Divine Power

The Omnipotent God who determines all with an unthwartable will begs Hartshorne's well-founded question: "Can we worship a God so devoid of generosity as to deny us a share, however humble, in determining the details of the world, as minor participants in the creative process that is reality?"[7] Of course we can't. Of course the loving divine power generously shares with us. It should be obvious that *humans* who exert their power over against other humans are atrocious. Unless we think the divine love is that kind of atrocity, of course the Omnipotent God is an incoherent view of God to which we must no longer assent.

Even Thomas Aquinas wrestles with what we really mean in suggesting that God is omnipotent. He doesn't want to look ridiculous, but "if, however we were to say that God is omnipotent because He can do all things that are possible to His power, there would be a vicious circle in explaining the nature of his power. For this would be saying nothing else but that God is omnipotent, because He can do all that he is able to do."[8] In other words, we are right to ask, *what is gained by affirming that the circle is round because the circle is round*? Our intellectual inheritance and potential as human beings created in the image of God deserves better than closed-circuit rationality.

It is time to remove from our understanding of divine omnipotence "absurdities of interpretation," as Tillich calls them.[9] Tillich goes on: "In popular parlance the concept of 'omnipotence' implies a highest being who is able to do whatever he wants."[10] Such an unanalyzed sense about God cer-

7. Hartshorne, *Omnipotence and Other Theological Mistakes*, 16.

8. Thomas Aquinas and Kreeft, *Summa of the Summa*, 182 (25:3).

9. Tillich, *Systematic Theology*, 1:278.

10. Ibid., 1:273.

tainly counts as a logical absurdity—but it is one so many people live with as an unquestioned general idea. So many of us persist in perverse notions of power because, in the words of Teilhard, "the heart cannot find complete rest in a God whom it does not feel to be stronger than anything that exists."[11] That comment brings to mind an aspect of truthiness we have so far mainly neglected. Of course we have been highlighting the dehumanizing divide that wrenches apart head and heart. But, according to Colbert, there is a second definition of truthiness. In fact, in an interview on December 25, 2016, on *Face the Nation*, more than two years out of character (having left his bombastic political pundit persona behind), the *real* Stephen Colbert reminisced about how he "coined this word called truthiness about how—preferring to believe what feels true to you rather than what you know the facts to be . . ."[12] Surely we all have *some* preferences that ignore the truth. But, the mistake is to give in to the impulse to assent to the bizarre theory that the Omnipotent God, to be worthy of worship, must be some kind of *absolute irrefutable strength*.

Even Aquinas, the clear champion of a *very* powerful God, will not allow us to deteriorate into silliness. So, he writes, "everything that does not imply a contradiction in terms, is numbered amongst those possible things, in respect of which God is called omnipotent: whereas whatever implies contradiction does not come within the scope of divine omnipotence, because it cannot have the aspect of possibility."[13] Any high school theology teacher will have to admit that not a semester will go by without someone trotting out the favorite sixteen-year-old logical triumph against the Omnipotent God: *They say for God to be omnipotent means God has to be able to create a rock so heavy that God cannot lift it.* That is exactly the "absurdity in interpretation" that Aquinas and Tillich and others warn against.

At this point we should take account of what has been said so far about the divine omnipotence. Certainly, it cannot be taken to mean that God alone has all the power and does not share it to any degree, because that would mean there is no such thing as creaturely freedom—and without freedom, meaning and responsibility are erased. Dionysius the Areopagite points out how silly it is to imagine a God who hoards all the power, since "this distribution of God's Infinite Power permeates all things, and there

---

11. Teilhard de Chardin, *Christianity and Evolution*, 29.

12. Dickerson, "Face the Nation Transcript."

13. Thomas Aquinas and Kreeft, *Summa of the Summa*, 182 (25:3).

is nothing in the world utterly bereft of all power."[14] To be utterly bereft of power means to be nothing—or quite literally to be no thing. Furthermore, omnipotence cannot be taken to mean the absurdity of circular logic, or the logical absurdity of God doing what cannot be done. Aquinas is also aware of what Teilhard worries about: that God must be powerful *enough* to warrant our worship and our confidence. But, Aquinas is so careful, and wishes to thread the needle: "it is better to say that such things cannot be done, than that God cannot do them."[15]

By qualifying omnipotence in these ways, does this make God unworshipable, unlovable? Hardly. In fact, we are *required* to reconsider divine omnipotence when we realize that the tyranny of a divine bully God who hoards power, imposing everything by an unquestionable will, is the furthest thing from love. Likewise, when we consider the God who endows humans with critical intelligence, it is an absurd offense to imagine that we are allowed to use our brains in every case *except* unintelligible ideas about God's power and love.

Hartshorne's helpful little book *Omnipotence and Other Theological Mistakes* recognizes that this thinking will face harsh criticism from the theological establishment, who "are likely to object to the new theology that it fails to acknowledge 'the sovereignty of God.' To them we may reply, 'are we to worship the Heavenly Father of Jesus (or the Holy Merciful One of the Psalmist or Isaiah), or to worship a heavenly king, that is, a cosmic despot?'"[16] This is certainly a clearly defined choice. And it will not be possible to reside in a muddled middle ground, worshipping a *merciful despot*, for instance, because what the devil could that possibly mean? *Merciful despot* is the sort of truthy concoction that should make your head hurt and your heart sink. A despotic God (even a merciful despot) who exercises *rigid power over against* much less powerful creatures—or even, utterly powerless creatures—is a tragic truthy idol. That God demonstrates the weakest kind of strength. It is a false power. A false strength. A fraudulent love. We *know* this.

What is more cowardly and horrifying than the wicked exercise of power by a man who beats his children and his wife? Maybe he appears to be "stronger" than the woman and the children. Look again. Domestic abuse is a destructive, worthless power. It is a failed power that reveals a

---

14. Dionysius the Areopagite, *Dionysius, the Areopagite*, 156.

15. Thomas Aquinas and Kreeft, *Summa of the Summa*, 182 (25:3).

16. Hartshorne, *Omnipotence and Other Theological Mistakes*, 14.

lack of power. Certainly the divine power we call love cannot be like abusive, fraudulent strength. Or, what is more cowardly and horrifying than the violent power of the terrorist or the hate-criminal who destroys the lives of innocents, inflicting terror in the survivors? Certainly the divine power we call love cannot be like terrorizing, fraudulent strength. Divine omnipotence is divine truthiness at every turn because it produces an incoherent riddle between God's power and God's love. If we want to retain the idea of God's omnipotence (and we really might want to), going forward it will have to mean that God's power fully harmonizes with God's love.

Chapter 19

Not the End of (the List of) Divine Truthiness

O f course, these are not all of the wrong, dangerous, and truthy ideas about divinity, deity, ultimate reality, originating reality, *God*—but at least this is a good start. It may be helpful to see again, but condensed all in one place, the notions of God that we are calling *divine truthiness*. The truthy God is:

1. Imperial Ruler in the Cult of Onlyness

2. Impassible

3. Absolute Moralist

4. Statically Perfect Unmoved Mover

5. Supreme Owner

6. Literally Male

7. Omnipotent

To that list we have added the divine truthiness that insists on a literal reading of the Bible, since that method of interpretation is an insidious support mechanism for the truthy God. Each of these is divine truthiness because each of these notions separately, and taken as a whole, are examples of how words about God (theology) become incoherent—examples of how truthy dogmatism enforces the split of thoughtful minds from sensitive hearts. They are truthy junk thought because they propose a violent and hateful divine power that excels in creating victims and executioners. That truthy power makes God's love into a fraud.

With these examples in hand, what is needed is a way to honor the head-and-heart truth that God must be love with the head-and-heart truth that God must also be powerful. Divine truthiness reigns whenever God's love is maligned by perverse power. Divine truthiness reigns whenever we are asked to check our brains at the door. Divine truthiness reigns whenever we are asked to ignore our hearts, our feelings.

Perhaps this part of the book has felt like a long complaint. If that's the case, never fear: there is hope. The rest of the book is dedicated entirely to building up an informal interreligious constructive theology that honors both head and heart. In the rich and robust spiritual inheritance that courses through history to our beating hearts and inquiring minds, we will at last be able to describe real power that energizes real love.

Holding up Buddhism, Christianity, and Taoism together is not implying these three religions are saying the "same thing" about power. That would be absurd and truthy. But the hope is to be able to recognize a dynamic mutual corroboration when seemingly divergent traditions are able to move in similar directions. For instance, a Christian can be encouraged when she can recognize deep resonances between Christianity and Taoism or Buddhism. It can be comforting to discover gentle harmony among the revelation of the Christ, the words of the *Tao Te Ching*, and the Buddha's teaching about the Tathata of reality. It does not have to be a challenge or defeat of anyone's personal religion to discover that others' wisdoms flow on a familiar current.

Clearly, we should not underestimate the influence of divine truthiness. The grip it has on our imaginations and our theology and our anthropology is strong. We will not overcome it by some force of will, because to attempt to do so is just a backdoor reinforcement of the regime of coercive compulsion! When we set our will to overthrowing the imperial, coercive, and tyrannical deity, we in the very act double down on our faith in the effectiveness of coercion as a technique for achieving our goals. The shock of the irony should get us to take notice. We must rather allow the simple and soft truth of authentic love-power to melt away these faulty notions. A rich plethora of Buddhist, Christian, and Taoist wisdom will converge to give us hope that another way is possible. All these complaints about divine truthiness can be transformed into a powerful and loving replacement. The following chapters construct a gentle and humane theology of wholeness that honors the divine power and divine love, without conflict. Actually, if omnipotence is the divine power of love, then maybe that's a definition that will make it possible to keep the term *omnipotence* (see chapter 20). We are at long last leaving behind and replacing divine truthiness with something better: the divinity who is powerful love.

Part 4

Tathata-Tau-Tao Power

. . . violence is not strength and compassion is not weakness.[1]
ALAN JAY LERNER

Take a Breath

It is my great hope at this point that you will take a deep breath with me. A real breath. Please breathe in deep and relax a moment. A journey that is all work and no delight is hardly worth the trouble. Maybe you will even just rest a little while, follow your breath, and feel yourself being supported by the chair, the bed, or the airplane where you are reading. Follow your breath without following your breath, so your breath can follow you, and you can see that no one is leading—you're just breathing. There is space for your life, air for you to breathe, and lungs for the breathing. Space. Breath. Life. What greater delight do we need?

***

I do hope you did pause, and if you didn't yet, I hope that you will reconsider, and take the opportunity now. And even if you did, you may wish to linger a little longer. And that would be just fine.

***

1. Lerner, *Camelot*, 70.

Breathing gives us a moment to recall the discoveries we have already made on the road to end divine truthiness. We have met fellow travelers who have joined us along the way. With them we sing in a chorus, a new and rising harmony that has for so long whispered in the background—so quietly we could barely hear. Of course divine truthiness has been too long shouted from the mountaintops. And the shouting wastes so much breath. So loud is divine truthiness that it cannot be ignored, and so we have met with its incoherencies. But we must not stop there. We scatter the power of divine truthiness by redirecting its force. See it stumble. See it crumble beneath its own weight.

Because of our forays into divine truthiness, we are equipped and motivated for this next stage of our passage. We are motivated to encounter the genuine power that is love, the loving power of divinity. With the problems clearly defined, we are free to see a new way emerging. Actually, it is not really a new way. It is just a way whose travelers were separated, whose path was obscured. Now that we are familiar with the truthy obstacles, we can better see the other way emerge: a way of confidence and honesty, a way of power and love: the God who is truly God is the God who is truly love. And the God who is truly love is the God whose power consists of love.

We are in a position at last to recognize, on the one hand, that "everything is wrapped in an utter relativity of radical interdependence because every being is a function in the hierarchical order of beings and has its own place in the dynamism of history, a place not incidental to the thing but actually making the thing what it is."[2] And on the other hand, we can finally banish the truthy notion that hierarchical order is about authoritarianism, rank, and domination. *Real reality* demonstrates the firm and delicate interrelation of mutuality, where the processes of existence whisper the truth of God and world together in harmonious becoming. Imagine a mindset of holistic continuity from highest divinity to most trifling wisp of reality. An integrated and holistic approach like that can grant us confidence to seek truth in a wider path. And a wide path can accommodate walking partners and friends. A Christian accompanies a Buddhist. A Taoist walks with a Christian. All three can join hands without fear—confident in powerful love.

Friends sharing the journey is really an excellent image for what I hope to accomplish. This is not the time for angry disputation and triumphalism. In the coming pages, I really ask the reader to allow us to move

2. Panikkar, *Intrareligious Dialogue*, 5.

freely among these three religions. The goal is not doctrinal rigidity. The goal is not dogmatic certainty. The goal is not to develop a treatise on these three religions that accounts for all they have to say. The goal is to find in them precious clues about an alternative type of power that is compatible with love. The goal is to engage our whole heart and our whole mind so that these three religions can teach the best wisdom they have to offer. The goal is to uncover harmonious language that points us to loving power that animates each of these religions. Buddhism gives us the symbol of *Tathata*, the suchness of the power inherent in things as they are. Christianity gives us the symbol of *Tau*, the authentic divine power of the cross. Taoism gives us the symbol of *Tao*, the power of the Way. To replace fraudulent power that ruins love, to replace divine truthiness, we turn to Buddhist *Tathata*, Christian *Tau*, and Taoist *Tao* (the Suchness, the Cross, the Way). With Tathata-Tau-Tao as our guide, we will come to know the gentle impress of another way: *the power of love without contradiction.*

Chapter 20

Buddhist Power:
Tathata of Tathata-Tau-Tao

Tathata Is the Power of Mutual Becoming:
The Buddha's Interdependent Co-Arising

In this journey to end divine truthiness, you may have noticed there's no escaping the Buddhist idea Tathata. And it will therefore be no surprise that here we are returning to Tathata again. Because we have already been using this idea as a thoroughly Buddhist contribution that has many analogues in many realms of learning, I hope you will not be alarmed that this chapter will playfully expand our idea of Tathata.

Why spend so much time on this idea of mutual becoming as the Tathata of reality? The energy and attention are meant to counteract the vast, rigid, and harmful regime of divine truthiness with its gospel of radical separation. Wrong ideas of hyper-independence cut each creature off in harmful and destructive ways from their true nature, which is interconnection, interdependence, and mutuality of becoming. We in the US are so used to hallowing the supreme individual that we need lots of practice recognizing the solidarity of mutuality. And *mutual becoming* is just a way of describing the Tathata of reality, the *pratitya samutpada*, which is the pinnacle of the Buddha's enlightened wisdom. As we have already seen, the Buddha teaches:

> This being, that becomes;
>> from the arising of this, that arises;
> this not being, that becomes not;
>> from the ceasing of this, that ceases.[1]

---

1. Macy, *Mutual Causality in Buddhism*, 39.

If I may be permitted, I think the truth underlying that teaching may also be stated like this:

> When this becomes, that becomes,
>> with the mutual arising of this, that mutually arises.
>
> When this does not become, that does not become,
>> with the cessation of this mutual becoming, that mutual becoming ceases.

In the constant flow of change, each new manifestation of each element of creation is utterly dependent upon all that came before it. It depends on the self-relinquishment, the self-giving, the self-donation of every previous manifestation that gives way to make room for the new. To speak in terms of Tathata, the fact of the power of mutual becoming that makes everything make itself is the reality of *pratitya samutpada*, or the interdependent co-arising of all phenomena. Tathata teaches that the real power of reality is the power of mutual becoming.

Since interdependent co-arising is true, it is not only a Buddhist insight. Since we have been dwelling with this idea of Tathata for so long already in this book, we are free to see how the mutual becoming of reality really works, outside the walls of Buddhism. Clearly, not only Buddhists can recognize Tathata as the radical and comprehensive web of interrelation where every cause is simultaneously effect, and where there is a relative infinity of causes for each unique creature in the multiplicity of being. The Buddha's insight is a human insight. So, it is unsurprising to hear an early Christian theologian, Irenaeus of Lyons, say something similar as he marvels at the variety of creation:

> Created things, in their great number and diversity, fit beautifully and harmoniously into the creation as a whole. And yet, when viewed individually, they appear discordant and opposed to each other, just as the sound of the lute makes a single harmonious melody out of many and opposite notes by means of the intervals between them. [2]

Arising in a treatise against Gnostic heretics, Irenaeus's second-century language of music and the beauty of chords is an eloquent example in an early Christian context of the notion of *pratitya samutpada*, which permeates all authentic Buddhist *dharma* (teachings). Similarly, in the twentieth century the Roman Catholic Cardinal Walter Kasper suggests that "we define

2. Irenaeus of Lyons, *Scandal of the Incarnation*, 41.

our existence by what others are; our existence is essentially co-existence."[3] The co-existentialism of our reality is a way of agreeing that the Tathata of reality is mutual becoming, interdependent co-arising of all. In a treatise on eschatology (words about the end of things), the Christian theologian Monika Hellwig describes mutual becoming in the general resurrection at the end of time as "the essential interrelatedness and community of destiny of all human persons at all times and places."[4]

These represent just one more sampling beyond the walls of Buddhism of a burgeoning sensitivity to the fact of Tathata, which is the power of mutual becoming. By now, it seems scarcely possible to embark on any branch of theology or science without acknowledging the growing awareness of the truth inherent in Buddhist Tathata, the mutuality of becoming that empowers everything. This insight is both succinct and immense: the only genuine power of reality is the power of mutual becoming. And that insight is the passionate heart and inquisitive mind of efforts to unravel the knots of divine truthiness.

Viewing the Tathata of reality makes it possible to imagine power that does not distort love into incoherent babble. The reassertion of the Tathata of reality is also a statement about divinity or ultimacy, since the creation is the sacrament of the divine reality. It is as simple as that. What has so long made that connection difficult to discern is insidious divine truthiness that maliciously disconnects the supposed unchanging permanent divine perfection from the imperfect change of everything else. When there is courage to set aside divine truthiness, the simple truth that the creation is a reflection of the creator can shine bright. Whitehead says it like this: "God is not to be treated as an exception to all . . . principles, invoked to save their collapse. [God] is their chief exemplification."[5] Whitehead is so right. *The divine reality is the chief exemplification of reality, not the chief exemption!* That kind of continuity from God to the universe finally makes it possible to imagine divine power in breathtaking accord with divine love. Divine power and divine love can be summed up with a new word for wholesome, empathetic love that is grateful and generous and that dances between solitude and solidarity. That word? *Omnicaritas.*

3. Kasper, *Jesus the Christ*, 202.

4. Hellwig, "Eschatology," 363.

5. Whitehead, *Process and Reality*, 343.

Omnicaritas Is the Source of Tathata

In the complaints about divine truthiness, we have already encountered many aspects of the long history of doctrines of divinity. For instance, we saw some of the negative doctrines (the *ims*) of static immutability (the impossibility of divine change) and impassibility (the impossibility of divine suffering), and we glanced at some of the positive doctrines (the *omnis*), things like omniscience (God is all-knowing), omnipotence (God is all-powerful), and omnipresence (God is present everywhere). Of course, there are good and bad aspects to all these buzzword philosophical theologies. But isn't it fascinating that none of them take up *love* as the basic way to understand God?

The new *omni* does just that. It affirms that God is all-loving, that God is *Omnicaritas*, where Omni means "all," and caritas means "love." The love known as caritas (usually translated as charity) is active love given to benefit the other with no regard for whether the recipient deserves or merits the gift. Caritas means pure, gifted, universal love without conditions. The explicit intention behind this new word points both to the *love* and to the *all*. Don't underestimate the all. Discussions about perfect divine love need to be discussions about divine *perfectioning* that focus on perfecting loving, which flows and grows and adapts, rather than on static, completed perfection. Tillich has a helpful insight in his book *Christianity and the Encounter of the World Religions*: "it is significant that the famous words of Jesus, 'You, therefore, must be perfect, as your heavenly Father is perfect,' (which has always been an exegetic riddle) would . . . be better translated, 'You must be all-inclusive as your heavenly Father is all-inclusive.'"[6] Perfect love is divine love, and divine love is all-inclusive of an ever-expanding reality. That means *Omnicaritas* is also never static, but always expanding, always accommodating the new. The statement "God is love" (1 John 4:8) is a confident declaration that God is *Omnicaritas*. Love understood that way means it is possible to take the words of Jesus *be perfect as your heavenly Father is perfect* as the most basic calling: *live out the Omnicaritas*. Live out Omnicaritas by making your love all-inclusive, too. The divine Omnicaritas calls out to people to enact to the best of their ability an inclusive love for which Jesus gives a great symbol: *to love even the enemy* (Matt 5:43–45).

---

6. Tillich, *Christianity and the Encounter of the World Religions*, 35–36.

Divine Omnicaritas is the permanent challenge against divine truthiness. To prevent love from being submerged in incoherence and perversion, divine power and divine love must mutually support one another.

Divine love dwells in all creatures as their power to exist, and accompanies them as their support and guide, gently calling them toward their finest possible future—but always, everywhere honoring freedom. If God is love, and God is omnipresent, then the divine love is everywhere empowering everything. And that is the meaning of Omnicaritas: God is the All-Love, present everywhere, always. In that regard, omnipotence means Omnicaritas, and affirms *one* literal reading of Scripture: God is love (1 John 4:8). When powerful divine love can be found in every place, the great news is we really can know something about divinity by knowing something about the world. Therefore, since mutual becoming is the Tathata of reality, the wisest answer is to cut away needless divine truthiness, and declare Tathata to be the surest sign of powerful divine love in creation.

Tathata Is Mutual Becoming Power
that Balances Stability and Freedom

Talking about loving power, or even any idea of force, does not have to degenerate into caricature. The mere fact of force of *any* kind does not immediately annihilate love. In fact, love requires some kind of basic stability in which to emerge. Total fluidity, total change, with no continuity from moment to moment, would be a kind of chaos where value cannot be built. But, total solidity with absolute conformity from moment to moment is a kind of frozen death where value cannot be increased. The *Rule of Saint Benedict*, which is the regulation of life according to which Benedictine nuns and monks orient their life, has at its core a notion of stability (it is one of their vows) with perpetual conversion. The end of the prologue states the situation well:

> Therefore we intend to establish a school for the Lord's service. In drawing up its regulations, we hope to set down nothing harsh, nothing burdensome. The good of all concerned, however, may prompt us to a little strictness in order to amend faults and to safeguard love. Do not be daunted immediately by fear and run away from the road that leads to salvation. It is bound to be narrow at the outset. But as we progress in this way of life and in faith, we shall run on the path of God's commandments, our hearts overflowing with the inexpressible delight of love. Never swerving from his instructions,

then, but faithfully observing His teaching in the monastery until
death, we shall, through patience, share in the sufferings of Christ
that we may deserve also to share in His kingdom. Amen.[7]

Does it immediately offend a modern mind that one might agree to live life
according to regulations in a *school for the Lord's service*? Maybe. But, the
truth is all people are members of one community or another (as well as
members of total community of the universe), and the basic requirement of
social existence is consent to some impulse regulation. Obeying stop signs
saves lives. Life on Earth is only possible due to the stabilizing rule of gravity. Every human thought is the gift of oxygenated blood, which requires
atomic and molecular bonds. This is because that is: Tathata is the *rule* of
mutuality of becoming.

Benedict is recognizing nothing more than the miraculous gift of
"stability in the community,"[8] which provides the bedrock basis for the
shift from *regulatory commandments* to *the inexpressible delight of love*.
That is why the three vows the Benedictine monk makes are "promises
[of] stability, fidelity to monastic life, and obedience."[9] In other words, the
Benedictine vows are *stability, stability-in-transformation*, and *stability-in-
action*. They are vows that place the one who promises them firmly in the
Tathata of the persistent, permanent turbulence of transient impermanence
and the fluency of mutual becoming.

Another helpful lens for viewing stability comes from Serene Jones.
When she applies feminist principles to Christian theology, Jones talks about
bounded openness.[10] Mere absolute fluid openness risks everything to the
whim of anarchy. Meanwhile, mere absolute permanent boundedness is just
another name for slavery. The power of permanence requires the power of
fluency, and vice versa[11]—and a real violence erupts whenever these powers
are bereft of each other. *Bounded openness* describes Tathata well.

Stability can also be viewed through the work of scientists who have
observed what has been called the *finely tuned universe*, with the four
fundamental forces—gravitational, weak nuclear, strong nuclear, and elec-
tromagnetic—and a rate of universal expansion so precise that were any
of these regulating forces differently calibrated by the smallest degree, the

7. Benedict of Nursia, *RB 1980*, prologue, 45–50.

8. Ibid., 4:78.

9. Ibid., 58:17.

10. Jones, *Feminist Theory and Christian Theology*, 152.

11. Whitehead, *Process and Reality*, 347.

Tathata of our mutually becoming universe would have failed to manifest. Even apart from the breathtaking stability of precision, the mere fact of the existence of laws or rules of nature at all is a marvel. What's perhaps more astonishing than the mere fact of laws of nature is something religious people have long known, and science is now beginning to express as well: there is real freedom rather than total determinism.

Freedom within the stability of regulation is the only kind of freedom that can exist. The perfectly ordinary miracle of the universe lies in the divine providence of the general order within which creatures get to freely invent their mutual worlds. Avoiding the mere caricature of force reveals that the laws of nature are a kind of force that make mutual becoming possible; that make everything possible.

We may also view "stability" through the lens of cultural compulsion. Whitehead takes the more basic notions of *required stability in freedom*, *bounded openness*, and the *mutual becoming from the laws of nature* and applies them to "civilized communities," which he says *struggle* "with two kinds of compulsion. There are the natural necessities, such as food, warmth, and shelter. There are also the necessities for a coordination of social activities."[12] These necessary obligations are unavoidable manifestations of "the iron compulsion of nature."[13] But they are not evil in themselves. Without them, even life wouldn't be possible.

Taking all of these together—from Benedict, science, Jones, and Whitehead—discloses an underlying regime of stable order and regulated boundedness that provides the foundation for the miraculous and ongoing mutual becoming—a *permanence power* that issues forth in *fluency power* and freedom. In these ways, it is possible to observe the necessary and subtle *force* that is commensurate with authentic love, and that is actually a building block of love. Tathata is the power of mutual becoming in a universe where stability and freedom perpetually dance in creative tension.

Tathata Non-Violently Overcomes Fraudulent, Coercive, Divine Power

Even keeping the positive and necessary sense of force in mind shouldn't diminish vigilance against the harmful effects of the overemphasis on coercive divine power. Brute force, imperialism, militarism, and abuse are

12. Whitehead, *Adventures of Ideas*, 69.
13. Ibid., 85.

antithetical to love. Whitehead astutely describes how even though force can have "a benign effect so far as it secures the coordination of behaviour necessary for social welfare," that should not distract from the fact that "it is fatal to extend this dominion beyond the barest limits necessary for this coordination."[14] But dominion *far beyond the barest limits* is exactly what happens when truthy theology of divine domination prevails. It is then that we see the wages of the "reign of force" as it takes the form of "war, slavery, and governmental compulsion."[15] So, stay vigilant against the regime of divine truthiness. It has an insidious way of reinforcing itself.

The divine truthiness called *omnipotence* says God has, retains, and exercises *all* the power. But that leads back to the earlier question: who even wants an *all*-powerful God? Or, as Paul Sponheim asks, "can God have all the power, if we have some?"[16] Thankfully, the power of divine Omnicaritas isn't stingy. The kind of divine power that is consistent with Tathata does not come from an infinite insecurity that enforces its will on others. So much more marvelous is the God who can share in the delights and misfortunes of creatures. Divine love does not micromanage creaturely actions. Actually, even if it could micromanage them, it would not because divine love limits the divine power. What can divine limitation mean? Moltmann helps make this point: "if God *is* love, then his liberty cannot consist of loving or of not loving. On the contrary, his love is his liberty and his liberty is his love. He is not compelled to love by an outward or inward necessity. Love is self-evident for God."[17] And authentic love will not exceed the *barest necessary limits of compulsion*. Authentic divine love means enforcement is banished and replaced by invitation, call, and persuasion, where creatures have real say in what they become.

Tathata: Persuasion, Not Coercion

But does this all sound like postmodern liberal innovation? In the words of Keith Ward, "it raises the difficulty that it is hard to see how God can ever finally triumph, since God lacks finally decisive causality."[18] Are we so entrenched in the ruts of divine truthiness that we think offering a different

14. Ibid.

15. Ibid., 83.

16. Sponheim, *Love's Availing Power*, 38.

17. Moltmann, *Trinity and the Kingdom*, 151.

18. Ward, "The World as the Body of God," 70.

view of divine power means the ruination of God? Let's hope not. Actually, it is no new idea that genuine power doesn't have to mean coercive force. After all, it's kind of hard to level a charge of liberal innovation against Plato, who says, "The creation of the world" is best understood as "the victory of persuasion over force."[19] That means that this moment, now, is stable to the extent to which the past is a power reimposing its structure on the present. But, to be hemmed in by coercion on all sides, the past enforcing its structure and a deity implementing its will as the only possible future, drains all the meaning and responsibility out of existence. But that is divine truthiness. What a joy to meet the genuine God who works by persuasion, rather than coercion. What a joy to meet the God who lets creatures be creatures. What a joy to meet the God who is the supreme example of power consistent with genuine love, Omnicaritas. And that is the kind of power and love that can finally dispense with the truthy God. That is Tathata, the power of mutual becoming.

It turns out the Buddha is right about the Tathata of reality: interdependent origination power makes everything exist. With the inclusive horizon expanded, no one should again be required to resort to the puny, selfish, self-enforcing truthy divinity. But that doesn't mean God has been summed up. Buddhist Tathata is just our starting point. To continue the case studies of this minority report on the meaning of genuine divine power and love without contradiction, it is time to turn to the Christian symbol for divine power and love: the *Tau* of the Christ.

---

19. Whitehead, *Adventures of Ideas*, 83.

Chapter 21

Christian Power: Tau of Tathata-Tau-Tao

W hen faced with unfamiliar words, even in the title of this chapter, it is important to define them without much ado. While the word *Tau* is not actually *new*, it may be *new to you*. *Tau* is just the anglicized transliteration of the letter in the Greek alphabet *T* (uppercase) or *τ* (lowercase), and really it is just the letter that approximates the shape of the cross of Christ. It is that simple. Tau is just another word for the cross of Christ.

Saint Bonaventure uses the word *Tau* in his *Life of St. Francis*:

> For even while [Francis] lived among men, he imitated angelic purity so that he was held up as an example for those who would be perfect followers of Christ. We are led to hold this firmly and devoutly because of his ministry *to call men to weep and mourn, to shave their heads, and to put on sackcloth, and to mark with a Tau the foreheads of men who moan and grieve*, signing them with the cross of penance and clothing them with his habit, which is in the form of a cross . . .[1]

To be *marked with a Tau* is to live a life contrary to the powers of the world. It is to live a life of generous giving and relinquishment, rather than a life of greedy acquisition. It is to live a life of grateful reception, rather than entitlement. And remember, the reciprocity of empathetic love is composed of gratitude and generosity—both. It is to live a life of stable conformity to the example of Christ, the example of the cross of Christ. For Francis, such conformity to Christ's life and death is expressed as an "openhanded compassion for the poor . . . that had so filled his heart with generosity that . . . he determined not to be deaf to the gospel but to give to everyone who begged (Luke 6:30)."[2] To be *marked with the Tau* is to be marked with total

---

1. Bonaventure, *Bonaventure*, 181–82., (emphatic underlining mine).
2. Ibid., 186.

generosity toward the poor and total gratitude for the gift of the gospel. And to talk about generosity and gratitude means we are talking about genuine empathetic love.

Bonaventure also relates the second vision of Brother Pacificus, who "advanced in holiness; and before he went to France as provincial minister . . . merited to see a second vision: a *great Tau on Francis's forehead*, which shone in a variety of colors and caused his face to glow with wonderful beauty."[3] The Tau that shone with a variety of colors is the cross of Christ, the cross of inclusive love, the cross of generous giving. The *Tau of Christ*, or *Tau wisdom*, or simply *Tau*, are symbolic reminders to keep these references to Francis in mind. And Francis always points to the powerful love of Jesus Christ.

Tau Wisdom: Beware of Divine Truthiness

Tau wisdom is a difficult concept, but it is absolutely vital to understanding Christian thought. The Letter to the Colossians talks about how important it is to get Tau wisdom, or cross wisdom, correct: "See to it that no one captivate you with an empty, seductive philosophy according to human tradition, according to the elemental powers of the world and not according to Christ" (2:8). That statement is basically the same as the warning to be wary of the *empty, seductive philosophies* of divine truthiness. Tillich also advises caution: "the authority of Jesus the Christ is not the consecrated image of the man who rules as a dictator, but it is the authority of him who emptied himself of all authority; is the authority of the man on the Cross."[4] The *empty seductiveness* of divine truthiness lies precisely in the way it is embedded in deeply rooted, seemingly commonsense notions about what people ordinarily think real power is. Because Tau wisdom contradicts ordinary wisdom, it can be difficult to grasp.

In Christianity, there is no more central symbol than the cross, or Tau. The Tau is often regarded as a particularly distinctive aspect of Christianity in relation to other religions. Tau wisdom short-circuits divine truthiness notions about power by proclaiming, "power under weakness, . . . victory under defeat, glory under suffering, innocence under guilt, sanctity under sin, life under death" because it reveals to Christians that "the mystery of

---

3. Ibid., 214 (emphasis mine).
4. Tillich, *New Being*, 91.

salvation is the mystery of the child."[5] It is here that Christianity can offer an answer to divine truthiness.

To be forced to apply to God the worst aspects of human abuse of power—power-over-against a powerless other—is the worst sort of truthy mess. The book of James invites people to analyze wisdom in the activities of their lives:

> Who among you is wise and understanding? Let him show his works by a good life in the humility that comes from wisdom. But if you have bitter jealousy and selfish ambition in your hearts, do not boast and be false to the truth. Wisdom of this kind does not come down from above but is earthly, unspiritual, demonic. For where jealousy and selfish ambition exist, there is disorder and every foul practice. But the wisdom from above is first of all pure, then peaceable, gentle, compliant, full of mercy and good fruits, without inconstancy or insincerity. (3:13–17)

If it seems uncomfortable to believe God is *jealous* or has *selfish ambition*, please pay attention to that discomfort. It is uncomfortable for a reason: because it makes no sense. James is right: God's Tau wisdom and power are *peaceable, gentle, compliant,* and *merciful!* Jealousy and selfish ambition do not reveal God. Rather, they reveal some of the nastiest human vices. Elevating those vices as if they reflect divine love is a doomed effort of self-justification.

Tau wisdom reverses that faulty elevation. Moltmann agrees that the wisdom of Tau "sets out to liberate [people] from their inhuman definitions and their idolized assertions, in which they have become set, and in which society has ensnared them."[6] Tau wisdom is a liberating power that sets us free from divine truthiness. Moltmann goes on to say that "the one who knows God in the lowliness, weakness and dying of Christ does not know him in the dreamed-of exaltation and divinity of the man who seeks God, but in the humanity which he has abandoned, rejected and despised."[7] The imitation of God can't be allowed to degenerate into exaltation of the worst human vices. A true understanding of Tau wisdom reveals the thorny Christian truth that "God did not become man according to the measure of our conceptions of being a [hu]man. He became the kind of [hu]man we

5. Ibid., 95.

6. Moltmann, *Crucified God*, 72.

7. Ibid., 213.

do not want to be: an outcast, accursed, crucified."[8] Christianity's message for the world is surely *that* truth. The divine love-power is the kind that gets crucified because Tau wisdom is *peaceable, gentle, compliant,* and *merciful.*

The Pauline letters provide some of the best scriptural basis to understand Tau wisdom, and can help us probe the truth in Gospel writings. As Paul sees it, "the wisdom of this world is foolishness in the eyes of God, for it is written: 'He catches the wise in their own ruses'" (1 Cor 3:19). Don't get caught in the *ruses* of divine truthiness. It is precisely Tau wisdom that comes to the rescue. But that doesn't make it easy. The Gospel of Mark's account of Peter's faith confession illustrates the difficulty:

> Now Jesus and his disciples set out for the villages of Caesarea Philippi. Along the way he asked his disciples, "Who do people say that I am?" They said in reply, "John the Baptist, others Elijah, still others one of the prophets." And he asked them, "But who do you say that I am?" Peter said to him in reply, "You are the Messiah." Then he warned them not to tell anyone about him . . . He began to teach them that the Son of Man must suffer greatly and be rejected by the elders, the chief priests, and the scribes, and be killed, and rise after three days. He spoke this openly. (8:27–32a)

The confident Christian position of a twenty-first-century perspective regards this statement of Christ that he will die and rise as obviously self-evident. But, Mark continues the scene:

> Then Peter took him aside and began to rebuke him. At this [Jesus] turned around and, looking at his disciples, rebuked Peter and said, "Get behind me, Satan. You are thinking not as God does, but as human beings do." He summoned the crowd with his disciples and said to them, "Whoever wishes to come after me must deny himself, take up his cross, and follow me. For whoever wishes to save his life will lose it, but whoever loses his life for my sake and that of the gospel will save it." (8:32b–35)

Is it really so difficult to understand Peter's position? To Peter, Jesus' declaration about his upcoming execution seems senseless. Ordinary wisdom would assume that because Jesus is beloved by God the Romans would not be able to execute him. The commonsense appeal of a truthy notion of power makes it difficult for Peter to react in any other way. Peter is trapped by divine truthiness, and needs liberation. But, that liberation is so hard. Really, Peter is just a stand-in for the other people of his time—and ours—who are

---

8. Ibid., 205.

plagued by divine truthiness. And that's why Jesus asks the disciples to keep his identity as the *Anointed One*—or the *Christ*, or its Hebrew synonym, *Messiah*—a secret. Jesus knows that ordinary folks will immediately equate the wrong notions of power with the title *Messiah*. He knows they will think *Messiah* means a political, coercive, militaristic power, so he counsels that it's better not to use the term, so as not to invite the defective equation.

But, the equating of Messiahship (Christhood) with coercively mighty divine power doesn't go away when the Gospels are written down. Moltmann observes that "the religions and humanist world which surrounded Christianity from the very first despised of the cross, because this dehumanized Christ represented a contradiction to all ideas of God, and of man as divine."[9] When he says "and of man as divine" he means the theological anthropology that human beings are made in the image of God. The Apostle Paul agrees, saying, "Let no one deceive himself. If any one among you considers himself wise in this age, let him become a fool so as to become wise" (1 Cor 3:18). There is a genuine foolhardiness in divine truthiness, no matter how "obviously true" it seems. Tau is the cooling balm to heal the burn of divine truthiness.

The Christian effort to understand the event of Christ and the teachings of Christ is at the very core of Tau wisdom, which is a negation of conventional wisdom. The wisdom of the Tau actively negates divine truthiness in its various guises:

1. Imperial Ruler God in the Cult of Onlyness

2. Impassible God in the fear of change

3. Absolute Moralist God

4. Statically Perfect Unmoved Mover God

5. Supreme Owner God

6. Literally Male God

7. Omnipotent God

Jesus' own words announce the end of each of those: "Whoever wishes to come after me must deny himself, take up his cross, and follow me. For whoever wishes to save his life will lose it, but whoever loses his life for my sake and that of the gospel will save it" (Mark 8:34–35). Alas, maybe that should have been the end of divine truthiness right there . . .

9. Ibid., 40.

But, even eleven hundred years of people practicing to be good Christians didn't help much (and frankly, the last nine centuries haven't done much either). For example, the medieval saint Anselm of Canterbury (d. 1109) is genuinely mystified at how divine wisdom appears to be utterly senseless to human values, especially in how "God, in sparing the wicked, is just, according to his own nature, because he does what is consistent with his goodness; but he is not just, according to our nature, because he does not inflict the punishment deserved."[10] In much the same way, Aquinas marvels that "God acts mercifully, not indeed by going against His justice, but by doing something more than justice."[11] These great thinkers from the medieval church underscore the quandary of divine Tau wisdom. They emphasize that not even the passage of many Christian centuries can loosen the grip of divine truthiness over theology. Sadly, even today we are still in the grip of truthy ideas of power because it is so very difficult to come to terms with the fact that Tau wisdom is *peaceable, gentle, compliant,* and *merciful.*

The Right Kind of Humility to Understand Tau Wisdom

There is a true statement people say about God: *We are limited in our understanding, so we can never fully comprehend or express the immensity of God and God's ways.* The right kind of honest humility is in that statement.

But then something goes terribly wrong.

To say *God's wisdom is not human wisdom* is not an appropriate answer to the terrifying riddle that divine love supposedly acts violently. To say God's wisdom is not human wisdom is not the chance to rush in and equate the worst atrocities with God's love. It is not the opening to abandon all sense, throwing up our hands in helplessly limited understanding because we can never fully comprehend the immensity of God and God's ways. No. Love should be love. If it seems like violent hate, no one should be required to call it love.

Lots of Christians don't really know what's in their Bible. Though I hinted about this above in chapter 17, I think it might help to read a longer passage from Joshua, since I have the sense that plenty of Christians don't know this is in there:

10. Anselm of Canterbury, *Basic Writings*, 63.
11. Thomas Aquinas and Kreeft, *Summa of the Summa*, 169.

The LORD said to Joshua, "Do not fear them, for by this time tomorrow I will present them slain to Israel. You must hamstring their horses and burn their chariots." Joshua with his whole army came upon them suddenly at the waters of Merom and fell upon them. The LORD delivered them into the power of the Israelites, who defeated them and pursued them . . . They struck them all down, *leaving no survivors. Joshua did to them as the LORD had commanded*: he hamstrung their horses and burned their chariots . . . At that time Joshua, turning back, captured Hazor and struck down its king with the sword; for Hazor formerly was the chief of all those kingdoms. *He also struck down with the sword every person there, carrying out the ban, till none was left alive.* Hazor itself he burned. *All the cities of those kings, and the kings themselves, Joshua captured and put to the sword, carrying out the ban on them, as Moses, the servant of the LORD, had commanded.* (11:6–12; emphasis mine)

To read that the God who is love commands that human enemies must *all be put to the sword, and none left alive* should be scandalous. What is someone with a bright intellect and a tender heart supposed to do with that? The dangerous reaction to that incoherent biblical idea is to say that God's ways are "mysterious." The dangerous reaction to this incoherent biblical idea is to say that genocidal annihilation is part of the "loving plan" of the loving God, but we just don't understand it because we are limited humans with little human brains. The idea that God's love means the extermination of enemies is so horrible it results in unintelligible, incoherent babble: God's loving ways are mysterious . . . loving genocide must be divine wisdom. What? If love can mean genocide, then words no longer have meaning.

That can't be Tau wisdom. It is faulty *human* wisdom that calls for war. It is embarrassingly misguided *human* wisdom that thinks the murder of enemies is justifiable. Slaughtering every conquered human being cannot be the "hard to understand" divine way of "love." Mass murder and warfare are the worst atrocities of human beings. Here in the book of Joshua we see a prime example of how people fraudulently lift up the worst human atrocity to the status of God. In fact, Spong has lamented that "the list of objectionable passages could be expanded almost endlessly."[12] When we are forced to think that divine love requires genocide, the wholesome idea (that I can't box up God in my ideas because I can't fully fathom God) is twisted into a monster. That is a huge problem. That is divine truthiness invading

12. Spong, *Rescuing the Bible from Fundamentalism*, 20.

even the Bible. God does not command mass murder. And we know that because Tau wisdom is *peaceable, gentle, compliant*, and *merciful*.

Divine Self-Emptying (Kenosis)

One of the reasons divine truthiness continues to hold tight to the Christian imagination is, oddly, the doctrine that *in the incarnation God empties God's self*. This self-emptying is called *kenosis*. The word *kenosis* comes from the Greek word *kenoma*, which means "emptiness," the opposite of *pleroma*, which means "fullness." We find the main expression of kenosis in the Apostle Paul's Letter to the Philippians:

> Have among yourselves the same attitude that is also yours in Christ Jesus, Who, though he was in the form of God, did not regard equality with God something to be grasped. Rather, he emptied himself, taking the form of a slave, coming in human likeness; and found human in appearance, he humbled himself, becoming obedient to death, even death on a cross. (2:5–8)

Being stuck in divine truthiness can make it difficult to make sense of something like divine self-emptying. The language is stark: Jesus is God incarnate, *taking on the form of a slave, humbling himself* to the point of *accepting the humiliating death by crucifixion*. Distorted thinking may revolt against the possibility of the incarnation being like that. But, for a genuinely Christian perspective, in a way kenosis is the very wholesome meaning of incarnation. But, in another way the idea of kenosis can be contorted into perverse support for the truthy God.

How can kenosis-talk support divine truthiness? Here's how: To say that Christ *empties himself* seems to imply going from one state to another. It is precisely that idea which cements the notion of the exalted (all-mighty, imperial, truthy, etc.) God. That leads to the thought that somehow kenosis (self-emptying) is not an irreducible truth of divine love, but instead it is a characteristic secondary to the primary traits of high, exalted, mighty, imperial power that precede any emptying. But, Tau wisdom raises the alarm whenever a *theology of exalted might* arises. Kenosis, which is a function of divine logic and wisdom, cannot be taken to prop up divine truthiness, which is a function of ordinary logic or wisdom.

While so many Christians are satisfied to regard kenosis as a secondary feature of God, it takes a Zen Buddhist, Masao Abe, to discern the kind of kenosis essential to divine love. Abe uses unequivocal terms: "we should understand the doctrine of Christ's kenosis to mean that Christ as the Son of God is essentially and fundamentally self-emptying or self-negating—because of this fundamental nature, the Son of God is Christ—that is, the Messiah."[13] Kenosis is no secondary characteristic of Christ. It is *essential*, and *fundamental*. Abe argues that for those claims to be true the same must be true of God the Father: "without the self-emptying of God 'the Father,' the self-emptying of the Son of God is inconceivable."[14] With that, the insightful Buddhist in deep dialogue with Christians correctly links these claims to the truth of love.

Love based on conditions is something we humans do—not God. Every elevation of that conditional love to divine status is an act of idolatry. *Humans* can withhold love. *Humans* can grant love in measures more or less according to conditions. But, divine love (Omnicaritas, see chapter 20) isn't like that. Love that is divine doesn't stingily ration out love. Masao Abe couldn't be more correct: "If God is really unconditional love, the self-emptying must be total, not partial. It must not be that God becomes something else by partial self-giving, but that in and through total self-emptying God is something . . . "[15] Kenosis is not a derivative trait: kenotic self-emptying is who God is. And it is possible to go even further. The unconditional divine love does not withhold the divine presence from anyone—but rather pours out the divine presence in total generosity, holding nothing back. That is unconditional, self-emptying divine love.

That kind of total giving, total self-emptying, is the kind of kenosis that deserves to be emulated by beings created in the image of God. Saint Bonaventure writes about that endeavor to conform to God's love when he describes the life and death of Saint Francis of Assisi: "In all things he wished to be conformed to Christ crucified, who hung on the cross poor, suffering, and naked . . . O, he was truly the most Christian of men, for he strove to conform himself to Christ and to imitate him perfectly . . . and he merited to be honored with the imprint of Christ's likeness!"[16] That Franciscan conformity to Christ is conformity to self-emptying love. So important for Francis is the fact of Christ's crucifixion that this is a further

---

13. Abe, "Kenotic God and Dynamic Sunyata," 10.

14. Ibid., 14.

15. Ibid., 16.

16. Bonaventure, *Bonaventure*, 318.

meaning of kenosis, beyond the bare fact of incarnation. The utter self-giving of life in crucifixion can be understood as kenotic love—and that is Tau wisdom.

Tau Wisdom:
Paul, Moltmann, and the Holistic Theology of the Cross

For a Christian, a life that doesn't generously gift love to the neighbor might be stingy and faithless. It would be the opposite of Franciscan conformity to the Tau of Christ. A life without selflessness seems to show that one does not totally trust God. In place of trust, there is fear that withholds what the neighbor needs so fearful people can ensure their own selves will be safe. But, people are conformed to the Tau of Christ when selfless generosity of the divine love flows through them. It is only the person transformed by divine love who bears the boundless fruits of love: self-sacrificing-for-the-neighbor love; Tau love.

For the Christian imagination this selfless love is the natural outcome of the "theology of the cross." To understand that, an indispensable book is Moltmann's *The Crucified God*. In it he says a theology of the cross "is not a single chapter in theology, but the key signature for all Christian theology."[17] That means for Christians the Tau needs to be the preeminent, or even the only lens through which to look at any theological issue. *Theology of the cross* (i.e., Tau theology) is an organizing paradigm to make Christian sense of God, humanity, and the world.

Tau wisdom thus is meant to be a kind of holistic vision that is necessary to uproot the regime of divine truthiness. And Tau wisdom is realized when we recognize that through divine love God creates a world that reflects divine love and that is a further unfolding of divine love. Moltmann spells out what is at stake: "When the crucified Jesus is called the 'image of the invisible God', the meaning is that *this* is God, and God is like *this*. God is not greater than he is in this humiliation . . . not more glorious than he is in the self-surrender . . . not more powerful than he is in this helplessness. . . . not more divine than he is in this humanity."[18] That means Tau wisdom requires the idols of exalted power to be dissolved. The greatness of God only has meaning as humiliation. The glory of God only has meaning as authentic kenosis (and not as the kind of second-step kenosis that

17. Moltmann, *Crucified God*, 72.

18. Ibid., 205.

props up almightiness). The power of God only has meaning as weakness, as helplessness. Dietrich Bonhoeffer's words, quoted by Moltmann, leave no question about the seriousness and difficulty of this task:

> God let himself be pushed out of the world on the cross. He is weak and powerless in the world, and that is precisely the way, the only way, in which he is with us and helps us. Matt. 8.17[19] makes it quite clear that Christ helps us, not by virtue of his omnipotence, but by virtue of his weakness and suffering . . . only the suffering God can help . . . that is a reversal of what the religious man expects from God. Man is summoned to share in God's sufferings at the hands of a godless world.[20]

The chorus to end divine truthiness is singing Bonhoeffer's tune. It means *reversing what religious people expect of God*. It means dethroning divine truthiness that turns the worst traits of humanity into sacrosanct idols. Just as Buddhist Tathata (power of mutual becoming) banishes the false, coercive brands of power, so Christian Tau sends the truthy God (*Imperial, Impassible, Absolute Moralist, Statically Perfect Unmoved Mover, Supreme Owner, Literally Male, Omnipotent God*) packing.

In like fashion, yet another Lutheran, this time Tillich, says "the wisdom of this world in all its forms cannot know God, and the power of this world with all its means cannot reach God. If they try it, they produce idolatry and are revealed in their foolishness which is the foolishness of idolatry."[21] Tau short-circuits expectations. To paraphrase Mary's Magnificat (Luke 1:52), *Tau wisdom casts the all-mighty truthy idols from their thrones, and lifts up the power of lowliness.*

Here again is the Apostle Paul's idea that "The message of the cross is foolishness to those who are perishing, but to us who are being saved it is the power of God" (1 Cor 1:18). The death of the Son of God by crucifixion *is* the power of God. God's power *is* helplessness. *God is weak and powerless in the world.* It is possible to have the courage to let these truths once and for all dispense the truthy God to which so many people cling: the *Imperial, Impassible, Absolute Moralist, Statically Perfect Unmoved Mover, Supreme Owner, Literally Male, Omnipotent God.* Paul again:

---

19. Matt 8:17 says, "to fulfill what had been said by Isaiah the prophet: 'He took away our infirmities and bore our diseases.'"

20. Moltmann, *Crucified God*, 47.

21. Tillich, *New Being*, 112.

Consider your own calling, brothers. Not many of you were wise by human standards, not many were powerful, not many were of noble birth. Rather, *God chose the foolish of the world to shame the wise*, and God chose *the weak of the world to shame the strong*, and God chose *the lowly and despised of the world, those who count for nothing, to reduce to nothing those who are something*, so that no human being might boast before God. It is due to him that you are in Christ Jesus, who became for us wisdom from God, as well as righteousness, sanctification, and redemption, so that, as it is written, "Whoever boasts, should boast in the Lord." (1 Cor 1:26–31; emphasis mine)

The danger with words like these is when they are taken to imply that God is engaging in a kind of actual battle: the foolish shame the wise; the weak shame the strong; and the nothings reduce the somethings. The danger is believing this is just another run-of-the-mill justification for a role reversal where the oppressive regime proceeds unabated, only under new management. But these dangers are only possible when the insight of Tau wisdom is forgotten. In fact, it is only possible by omitting the context of the previous verse: "For the foolishness of God is wiser than human wisdom, and the weakness of God is stronger than human strength" (1 Cor 1:25). This divine wisdom is Tau wisdom, the *message of the cross*. And it does not merely reverse the roles of oppressor and oppressed. Tau wisdom erases the whole logic of oppression. Enforced power has nothing to do with divine love. And so it should have nothing to do with human beings who are created in the divine image. It should have nothing to do with the human impulse to conform to the highest Good—*the authentic God of powerful love*.

McDaniel learns the lesson of Tau wisdom, which is that "like Jesus on the cross we do not respond to violence with violence; rather, we respond to violence with love."[22] That is the language of divine love, where power aligns perfectly with love. According to Tau wisdom, for divine love to flower in human existence requires a power that completes love, rather than one that ruins it. Divine love is only meaningful in hearts and minds when it is acknowledged that in fact "power is made perfect in weakness" (2 Cor 12:9). The Apostle Paul's *power is made perfect in weakness* precisely because he is graced by God. There it is! That is the distilled meaning of Tau wisdom: love is made perfect in self-emptying generosity without remainder when *power is made perfect in weakness*.

22. McDaniel, *With Roots and Wings*, 57.

Tau Power: The Life, Teaching, and Death of Jesus

Power Perfected in Weakness, Vulnerability, and Retreat: Jesus' First Days

This other kind of power, the *power perfected in weakness* that appears as powerlessness, humility, self-emptying, and non-violence, makes genuine empathetic love possible. In a Christian view, this *power perfected in weakness* is embodied in the life, teaching, and death of Christ. In a Christian view, the divine power that saves comes in the unlikely form of a powerless baby. In the person of Jesus, love comes into the world as the *power perfected in weakness, the weakness of literal infancy* (Matt 1:25; Luke 2:11–16). In the person of Jesus, love comes into the world as the *power perfected in weakness* of vulnerability. The divine power comes to earth in *perfected weakness* of an infant who is vulnerable to the tyrannical power of Herod, who threatens Jesus' life. The Gospel of Matthew expresses *divine love as the power of vulnerability* in the story of how Jesus (the incarnation of God), his mother Mary, and his father Joseph flee as refugees to Egypt from the brutal, fearful power of Herod (Matt 2:13–20). When love comes into the world in the person of Jesus, its first status is the weakness of infancy; its second status is vulnerability to political power; its third status is that of a refugee in flight. According to the Christian view, *that* is what divine power looks like: infantile weakness, vulnerability, and retreat.

Or do we somehow still imagine that God is more like Herod? Do we imagine that Herod's enforcement of brutal power to slaughter innocents is more godlike than the power perfected in weakness of infancy, vulnerability, and retreat? Divine truthiness aligns divine power to Herod's brutality instead of the infantile weakness, vulnerability, and retreat of Jesus. Perish the thought. The truth is this: *power is perfected in infantile weakness; power is perfected in vulnerability; power is perfected in retreat.* Why is that so hard to accept? Because we are so infected by divine truthiness. And we worship the impotent truthy God instead of the God of whose power is genuine, empathetic love *perfected in weakness.*

Power Perfected in Weakness: Three Temptations

The story of the three temptations at the start of Jesus' public life demonstrates again the sharp contrast between two kinds of power. The truthy power of the tempter is displayed in the nature of the temptations themselves. In the effort to corrupt Jesus, the truthy tempter relies on the seemingly obvious ideas of authoritarian power embedded in divine truthiness. According to Luke's account, "Filled with the Holy Spirit, Jesus returned from the Jordan and was led by the Spirit into the desert for forty days, to be tempted by the devil. He ate nothing during those days, and when they were over he was hungry. The devil said to him, 'If you are the Son of God, command this stone to become bread'" (Luke 4:1–3).

In the first temptation of Christ, according to the internal logic of the story and ordinary truthy ideas about what divine power means, it seems Jesus is presented with a real option to forcefully overcome the nature of the stones, but for some reason he chooses not to. But, for the true divine *power perfected in weakness*, there really is no alternative but to allow the stones to be stones. Jesus refuses to imitate the truthy Omnipotent Imperial Enforcer God, because that would be idol worship. Stones should be allowed to be stones. Real love-power lets stones be stones. He's not tempted.

In the second temptation of Christ, the truthy tempter in Luke goes on:

> Then he took him up and showed him all the kingdoms of the world in a single instant. The devil said to him, "I shall give to you all this power and their glory; for it has been handed over to me, and I may give it to whomever I wish. All this will be yours, if you worship me." Jesus said to him in reply, "It is written: 'You shall worship the Lord, your God, and him alone shall you serve.'" (4:5–8).

And here Jesus is offered precisely the power of Herod, the power of Caesar, imperial power of glory, domination, and force. Of course, the central factor seems to be idolatry—Jesus will not worship the tempter, who is not God. But, recall the central insight against all the examples of divine truthiness: they are all forms of idolatry; where power destroys love, and one idolatry leads to another. The brute-force imperial power of tyranny is no less an idol than the tempter. Jesus' dismissal of false power is a double dismissal of double idolatries. Jesus won't worship the truthy God. He's not tempted.

The third temptation is for Jesus to attempt suicide, which would allegedly force angels to rescue him:

> Then he led him to Jerusalem, made him stand on the parapet of the temple, and said to him, "If you are the Son of God, throw yourself down from here, for it is written: 'He will command his angels concerning you, to guard you,' and: 'With their hands they will support you, lest you dash your foot against a stone.'" Jesus

said to him in reply, "It also says, 'You shall not put the Lord, your God, to the test.'" (4:9–12)

It might be more difficult to see how this temptation fits with the other two. What can it mean in the context of the story of Christ whose life *is* violently taken in the crucifixion, which is *not* prevented by any supernatural angelic intervention? Maybe the fact that angels do not intervene to prevent the crucifixion is just evidence of how genuine divine power simply does not enforce the divine will on creation. Maybe it is evidence of how God does not coercively and supernaturally overturn the power of mutual becoming— the Tathata—of the beloved universe. To read the third temptation like that, it fits with the first two: Jesus' love is the power that won't succumb to the absurd and truthy God. He is not tempted.

Taking all three together, Jesus exhibits, or *makes incarnate*, the *power perfected in weakness* of letting be; the *power perfected in weakness* called *non-imperialism*; and the *power perfected in weakness* that does not force the God of love to be the truthy God. These are just other names for *power perfected in weakness*, better known as love. They confirm that Tau wisdom is *peaceable, gentle, compliant*, and *merciful*.

Power Perfected in Weakness: Poor, Captives, Blind, Oppressed

Keeping with the Gospel of Luke, the first words of Jesus' public ministry are the following: "The Spirit of the Lord is upon me, because he has anointed me to bring glad tidings to the poor. He has sent me to proclaim liberty to captives and recovery of sight to the blind, to let the oppressed go free, and to proclaim a year acceptable to the Lord" (4:18). This now familiar Christian thinking is elsewhere stated more generically: *the last will be first and the first will be last* (13:30 et al.). Sadly this notion is still, in fact, *very* revolutionary because Christians have failed to make it reality. The problem is that Christians no longer hear Jesus' challenge. Instead, they think *we've heard it all before*. In the view of Jesus, the violently powerful are not powerful, because real *power is perfected in weakness*. In Luke's Gospel this framework (the first shall be last, etc.) of Jesus' life and mission is elegantly proclaimed in the voice of Mary, in her sublime Magnificat:

> "My soul proclaims the greatness of the Lord; my spirit rejoices in God my savior. For he has looked upon his handmaid's lowliness; behold, from now on will all ages call me blessed. The Mighty One

has done great things for me, and holy is his name. His mercy is from age to age to those who fear him. He has shown might with his arm, dispersed the arrogant of mind and heart. He has thrown down the rulers from their thrones but lifted up the lowly. The hungry he has filled with good things; the rich he has sent away empty. He has helped Israel his servant, remembering his mercy, according to his promise to our fathers, to Abraham and to his descendants forever." (1:46–55)

To read these words while thinking that God is like a Herod or a Caesar, we can be convinced that they confirm faulty and truthy theology. But, the divine overturning of the status quo described here—*He has thrown down the rulers from their thrones but lifted up the lowly. The hungry he has filled with good things; the rich he has sent away empty*—cannot be taken to mean violence. And neither does the phrase *He has shown might with his arm* indicate a violent, truthy, and loveless God. To think that these imply violence is to completely decontextualize the words, to do a kind of violence to them by ripping them from the Gospel. Jesus was born a weak infant into the status quo of an imperial power that immediately sought his death (something readers learn in Matthew's Gospel). Mary's words about social upheaval have to be aligned with Jesus' own words at the start of his ministry. They cannot be in mutual contradiction.

According to those words, Jesus is here to heal blindness, and liberate people from captivity and oppression. The false elevation of captivators, oppressors, and the enriched, as if they in some way are bearers of supposedly divine attributes, is the twisted logic of divine truthiness that impoverishes, imprisons, and oppresses people. Jesus' way of *power perfected in weakness* means that when love comes into the world its power proclaims *liberty to captives, recovery of sight to the blind,* and *frees the oppressed and impoverished* (Luke 4:18), *but not by creating new victims.*

The Good News cannot mean that there is a mere reversal of roles. The Good News cannot mean that the oppressed accept a promotion to be the new oppressor. The Good News is the undoing of oppressive structures by uprooting them, not by transplanting them. And this is the meaning of the beatitudes and the woes in the Lucan Gospel's depiction of the Sermon on the Plain:[23]

---

23. More commonly known as the Sermon on the Mount, as depicted in chapter 5 of Matthew's Gospel.

> Blessed are you who are poor, for the kingdom of God is yours. Blessed are you who are now hungry, for you will be satisfied. Blessed are you who are now weeping, for you will laugh. Blessed are you when people hate you, and when they exclude and insult you, and denounce your name as evil on account of the Son of Man. Rejoice and leap for joy on that day! Behold, your reward will be great in heaven. For their ancestors treated the prophets in the same way. But woe to you who are rich, for you have received your consolation. But woe to you who are filled now, for you will be hungry. Woe to you who laugh now, for you will grieve and weep. Woe to you when all speak well of you, for their ancestors treated the false prophets in this way. (6:20–26)

The wisdom of the world does not apply to the teaching of Jesus. His divine wisdom is Tau wisdom. Relying on common human understanding alone, it appears self-evident in the extreme that the poor are not blessed, and will continue to go hungry, while the weeping are given further reasons to grieve. And it likewise seems self-evident in the extreme that the rich have their consolation and should expect even more, the satisfied will be further satisfied, and those who laugh will be given further occasions for joy. Something more radical and fundamental than a violent role reversal is needed to overturn the establishment.

The liberation educator Paulo Freire has insightfully demonstrated that when oppressors are no longer able to keep oppressing, "the former oppressors do not feel liberated. On the contrary, they genuinely consider themselves to be oppressed. Conditioned by the experience of oppressing others, any situation other than their former seems to them like oppression."[24] In other words, the woes are only woes because of the removal of the advantaged status of being the oppressor. The loss of privilege *seems* oppressive, but it is not. Or at least it doesn't have to be.

The love-power of Tau taught and enacted by Christ is a radical egalitarianism famously described by the Apostle Paul: "There is neither Jew nor Greek, there is neither slave nor free person, there is not male and female; for you are all one in Christ Jesus" (Gal 3:28). When the rulers are cast down from their thrones, it is because the lowly have been lifted up—not because the rulers have been violently killed, and not because the lowly are replacement tyrants. When the rich are sent away empty, it is because the hungry have been at last filled, not because God requires a new class of hungry people. Their emptiness is only empty relative to their former

---

24. Freire, *Pedagogy of the Oppressed*, 39.

gluttony. And Freire would say, *conditioned by the experience of gluttony, any situation other than their former seems to them like starvation, but it is not.* They too will need to be fed.

Does this seem too convoluted? Are you somehow assured that God *must* wield the power of a tyrant? Are you certain God is really more like a Herod or a Caesar or a Job Creator—and therefore we are to read the statements that *He has shown might with his arm, dispersed the arrogant of mind and heart* and imagine that the God of love delights in humiliating his creatures? Do we read "He has thrown down the rulers from their thrones" and think the God of love enforces love by violence? Do we read "the rich he has sent away empty" and think the God of love enforces love by starving human beings? That is what a tyrant does. That is what a bully does. Not God, but an abuser humiliates. Not God, but an abuser withholds food. Certainly it is not the loving God who humiliates, abuses, and starves people. The truthy God is the abusive idol of perverse fantasies. The God of powerful love perfected in weakness is the only real God.

Don't forget how seductive this abuse theology is, though: if the worst aspects of humanity can be called "divine," then *Hallelujah!*, we are deftly absolved from the consequences of our terrible deeds. In fact, we find ourselves encouraged to engage in these supposedly godlike activities. How can that possibly be a legitimate way of doing theology? Are we so sure that God must *in the end* display the power of enforcement, because our truthy theology oppresses us with demons like a tyrannical god? Are we so sure that strength must mean power over, because otherwise we have some trouble seeing how God's love will win out in the end? If Tau is still hard to swallow, and if *power perfected in weakness* is still too hard to grasp by Jesus' words, then Jesus' actions are a further challenge—especially the manner of his death on the Tau, the cross.

Power Perfected in Weakness as Giving Way: Jesus' Crucifixion

The truest meaning of Tau wisdom is found precisely in the fact of the crucifixion. Despite the fact that we might think, *Yes, yes, I get it—I've heard about the cross all my life*, actually Tau wisdom remains very difficult. Paul says, "we proclaim Christ crucified," and this is "a stumbling block to Jews and foolishness to Gentiles" (1 Cor 1:23). That was a long time ago, sure, but it seems not to have gotten any easier. Tau wisdom eludes ordinary truthy wisdom. Tau wisdom *makes us stumble*, and *appears to be foolish*.

The Christian claim is that the victory of God is found in defeat. Here is paradox again. Ordinary truthy wisdom says that for God to allow the humiliating torture and crucifixion, he must hate Jesus. Tau wisdom is different. The example of the Tau displays weakness as the strongest most divine strength. But how?

The Christian belief is that *Christ is the fully divine and fully human Son of God.* In that confession seems to be the truthy implication that Christ had the "power" at his disposal to prevent his own crucifixion at the hands of the imperial Roman authorities. But that cannot be so. Divine love-power was not then, is not now, and won't ever be the kind that enforces, coerces, and violently compels. That conclusion is supported by the Gospel narratives, which talk about the simple fact that Jesus did no such thing. In the four Gospels, not only did Christ not prevent his own crucifixion by any act of violent force, but he did not even mount a verbal defense. Christ goes to his crucifixion in an act of total surrender, an act of non-resistance, an act of non-violence. The one who Christians call the Son of God exercises power that *gives in, gives way,* and *gives all.* The Apostle Paul says,

> . . . it is written: "I will destroy the wisdom of the wise, and the learning of the learned I will set aside." Where is the wise one? Where is the scribe? Where is the debater of this age? Has not God made the wisdom of the world foolish? For since in the wisdom of God the world did not come to know God through wisdom, it was the will of God through the foolishness of the proclamation to save those who have faith. (1 Cor 1:19–21)

In his effort to mine out the minority report that supports the wisdom of the Tau, Paul quotes Isaiah 29:14: "The wisdom of its wise men shall perish and the understanding of its prudent men be hid." The power demonstrated on the Tau is power that gives in, gives way, and gives all, because the divine love is *peaceable, gentle, compliant, and merciful power perfected in weakness.*

Furthermore, the resurrection of the Christ, which for Christians is the absolutely essential companion to the crucifixion, is not a display of blinding, deadly, violent retribution. The resurrection does not reverse the love and power we see in the Tau. Actually, the resurrection *confirms power perfected in weakness.* The resurrection appearances recorded in the Gospels don't talk about Jesus taking vengeance against those guilty of crucifying him. No. The resurrection appearances are about healing relationships, strengthening mutual bonds of love, and shedding light on the meaning of Christ's life and teaching. For instance, the Gospels depict Peter, the leader of the apostles, three times denying his friend Jesus in the hours before the crucifixion. Then, in a resurrection appearance, we see Jesus ritually healing and restoring his relationship with Peter:

> When they had finished breakfast, Jesus said to Simon Peter, "Simon, son of John, do you love me more than these?" He said to him, "Yes, Lord, you know that I love you." He said to him, "Feed my lambs." He then said to him a second time, "Simon, son of John, do you love me?" He said to him, "Yes, Lord, you know that I love you." He said to him, "Tend my sheep." He said to him the third time, "Simon, son of John, do you love me?" Peter was distressed that he had said to him a third time, "Do you love me?" and he said to him, "Lord, you know everything; you know that I love you." [Jesus] said to him, "Feed my sheep." (John 21:15–17)

Jesus heals the relationship by offering three opportunities for Peter to undo each of his three denials. The healing work of the resurrected Jesus is to give Peter the chance to replace each denial with a confession of love. We find out that Peter will be able to restore the relationship by lovingly caring for the metaphorical flock of Christ, the Good Shepherd. *That*, my friends, is the loving power of resurrection: resurrection power is new life where life has been lost. Resurrection power is new life for Christ, yes, but it is also new life for Simon Peter, and new life for the interrelationship between Jesus and Simon Peter. All of those lives are resurrected. And they are resurrected not by violence, but by the divine "mercy . . . from age to age" (Luke 1:50). So, it turns out resurrection *power perfected in weakness* is the same as crucifixion *power perfected in weakness*.

And if we think it would have been "possible" for Christ to act any other way, for God to act with some other kind of (violent, truthy) power, I say that can't be true. It is hard to imagine a more justifiable cause for a violent, vengeful return than that unjust and vile execution. If we believe theologies of divine truthiness, the resurrection event should have meant death to the executioners. But it did not. If we believe theologies of divine truthiness, the resurrection should have meant death, or some other punishment, to Jesus' denier, Peter. But it did not. And that is real evidence of the real character of divine power. Divine love-power cannot look anything like the power wielded by Herod or Caesar. It never has. It never will.

But, do we still think that the way of God will be to enforce some final vindication, some final vengeance at the end of time in the second coming of the Christ? If that were so, would not we have seen at least some smidgen of evidence of a vengeful, vindictive, coercive power in the resurrected Christ? It is time to drain the power of the disturbing influence of theologies of divine truthiness, theologies of the powerful Imperial Enforcer God whose will cannot and will not be thwarted in the end. Every time we assent to truthy notions of God, we must contend with divine love that is nonsensical: we wind up with a God whose power overcomes love in the end, whose love is enforced as violence.

It seems so much more Christian to take the stance that Christ *got it right the first time*—got it right in his teaching, on the Tau, and in the resurrection. What could be more irreverent than to look condescendingly upon the Christ who taught the release of captives and good news to the poor, refused the temptations of power, blessed the children, the poor, and the persecuted; met his own death with non-resistance; and resurrected to heal relationships? We should never have to shake our heads at the impracticality of the Jesus, whose *power is perfected in weakness*, whose wisdom is revealed in Tau and resurrection, and then turn around and declare that when he comes back—then, and only then—he will finally get it "right!" It is the definition of piety to say *Jesus got it right the first time*. I can't help but wonder if it isn't *embarrassingly* unchristian to imagine Christ's second coming as a reversal of the divine power revealed in the Jesus we meet in the Gospels. Doesn't it show far more humility to assume that Jesus really did get it right the first time, and the actual character of divine love and power are in total accord because power really *is* perfected in weakness? If the second coming of Christ is going to be a violent overthrow, then there's no hope for love.

The Love Revealed by a Suffering God— Not the Abusive Sky Parent

All this talk about the Cross, the Tau, means talking about how God suffers. And it is only with great care that divine suffering can be understood. There is a long, terrifying history of elevating suffering as if it were some sort of good in and of itself. Monica Coleman highlights the perverse abuse embedded in images of surrogacy, servanthood, and self-sacrifice when those ideas are applied to people who are already suffering.[25] The shadow side of emphasizing how the Son of God suffers without complaint is that it might

25. Coleman, *Making a Way out of No Way*.

seem to absolve oppressors. Is the unintended consequence to absolve the perpetrators of violence because they are providing an opportunity for victims to be sufferers who share in the suffering of Christ? Is an unintended consequence the blaming of victims for not being enough like Christ if they don't suffer in silence like he did? Those are deadly, dangerous perversions of Tau. Moltmann laments the fact that

> The church has much abused the theology of the cross and the mysticism of the passion in the interest of those who cause the suffering. Too often, peasants, Indians and black slaves have been called upon by the representatives of the dominant religion to accept their sufferings as 'their cross' and not to rebel against them . . . In a world of domination and oppression one must pay close attention to the concrete function of any preaching and any devotion."[26]

It is important to deal honestly with the outcomes of actions. No matter the intention, if the outcome of an action is the destruction of lives or the creation of suffering, that cannot be called love. The Tau wisdom that *power is perfected in weakness* is not permission to victimize others. Victimizers are not doing the "will of God" by creating suffering and death. But, if minds are infested with divine truthiness, people can be led down those dark, twisted rabbit holes.

The wrong views on the suffering of Christ have to do with doctrines about how it is that Christ "saves" by his death on the cross. Christianity is beset with a sometimes vague and sometimes dogmatic idea that God, the Father, desires and wills the suffering and death of the Son, Jesus Christ, for the salvation of the world. Terrifying images of an abusive Father God haunt the collective Christian imagination. The all-powerful Father God who is so impotent that love can only be expressed as torture and execution erases the meaning of love. The abusive parental God is the fraudulent truthy God. A mother's crying and falsely soothing words to her battered child, "*Your Dad doesn't mean to hurt you . . . Shhh . . . He loves you*," are the same kind of incoherent babble as theologies of the abusive sky Father whose absolute will is the suffering and death of his supposedly beloved Son. Divine truthiness elevates the divine abuser as if it were God. The abuser who is so impotent that he must require the violent death of his Son is not God.

---

26. Moltmann, *Crucified God*, 49.

Julian of Norwich Showing Power Perfected in Weakness as Divine Suffering Love

It is time to abandon the so-called God who is a supreme abuser. When we at last dethrone that truthy God, we are left with the question about how to make sense of the Tau, the suffering, and death of Christ. On the one hand, the suffering and death of Christ are the courageous display of divine love whose power does not shield itself from the pain of human tyranny. On the other hand, we cannot afford to romanticize suffering in a way that pardons perpetrators of violence. Is this too complicated? Are we trapped, stuck in an incoherent state of saying the God of love is also the opposite of love? Thanks to the medieval mystic Julian of Norwich, there is a way out of the trap.

In the mystical visions she calls her *Showings*, Julian deeply experiences the mystery of Tau. Make no mistake: these visions are an encounter with Christ in the most graphic, gory, and horrific detail of his crucifixion. So, on their surface, they seem at first to be in alliance with the divine truthiness of a God whose love is expressed in requiring his Son to suffer. But I am surprised to report that Julian's *Showings* actually tell of a tender sweetness of God's *motherly* love. To see only the horror show in Julian is to totally misunderstand her. But because it is so prominent, it can't be ignored. So, we start with the gore:

> And after this as I watched, I saw the body bleeding copiously in representation of the scourging, and it was thus. The fair skin was deeply broken into the tender flesh through the vicious blows delivered all over the lovely body. The hot blood ran out so plentifully that neither skin nor wounds could be seen, but everything seemed to be blood. And as it flowed down to where it should have fallen, it disappeared. Nonetheless, the bleeding continued for a time, until it could be plainly seen.[27]

Julian is shown *so much blood* in her visions. This is not just the blood that can pour out of a single human body. Julian depicts oceans and oceans of blood:

> Then it came into my mind that God has created bountiful waters on the earth for our use and our bodily comfort, out of the tender love he has for us . . . The precious blood of our Lord Jesus Christ, as truly as it is most precious, so truly is it most plentiful . . . The precious plenty of his precious blood overflows all the earth, and

27. Julian of Norwich, *Showings*, 199.

it is ready to wash from their sins all creatures who are, have been and will be of good will.[28]

This is enough blood to wash over all creatures, and envelop all of creation in blood. Beyond the bloody detail of the suffering of Jesus on the Tau, Julian takes the suffering even further. Her descriptions of the *drying* of the flesh in the wake of the bleeding are haunting. Here is a hint of it:

> I saw his sweet face as it were dry and bloodless with the pallor of dying, and then deadly pale, languishing, and then the pallor turning blue and then the blue turning brown, as death took more hold upon his flesh . . . Then I saw the sweet flesh drying before my eyes, part after part drying up with astonishing pain . . . the sweet body was so discolored, so dry, so shriveled, so deathly and so pitiful that he might have been dead for a week, though he went on dying.[29]

The dryness of death is a slow and increasingly painful and overpowering experience. These excerpted sections demonstrate how easy it would be to be trapped in the sensationalism of their impact. To be honest, in the first few reads of Julian it can be almost impossible to see past all the gruesome depictions. When they are all that can be seen it is easy to scoff at the seemingly ironic most famous line uttered repeatedly by Jesus in the *Showings*: "all will be well, and every kind of thing will be well."[30]

Thankfully, there *is* more to Julian than the masochism of physical suffering and wounds. It is in the *more* that Julian's genius rescues us from the fraudulent truthy God whose love is reprehensible abuse of the only Son. Julian observes, "This revelation of Christ's pains filled me full of pains . . . And in all this time that Christ was present to me, I felt no pain except Christ's pains . . . it seemed to me that my pains exceeded any mortal death."[31]

Let's stop right here, and emphasize the depth of that statement. When Julian empathetically enters into Christ's sufferings, she experiences the fact that she feels only the pain of her beloved, Christ. That leads her to ask, "Is there any pain in hell like this pain?"[32] Her question is like a cry: *how could the pains of hell be this bad?* Is there any pain in hell like the pains she experiences when her empathy embraces the pain of her beloved? But, her

28. Ibid., 200.
29. Ibid., 206–7.
30. Ibid., 225.
31. Ibid., 209.
32. Ibid.

question is not mere rhetoric. The showings are interactive. She receives an answer: "Hell is a different pain, for in it there is despair."[33] The pain in hell is not like the pain she is experiencing. What is the difference? Hell's pain is despair. So, her empathetic suffering is not like hell: the pain of her empathetic suffering is the pain that comes from genuine love—what Moltmann calls *suffering love*. She goes on, illuminating the height of the genius revealed to her:

> But of all the pains that lead to salvation, this is the greatest, to see the lover suffer. How could any pain be greater than to see him who is all my life, all my bliss and all my joy suffer? Here I felt unshakably that I loved Christ so much more than myself that there was no pain which could be suffered like the sorrow which I felt to see him in pain.[34]

Julian is brought back to this suffering and has a genuine illumination. She says that of all the pains that lead to salvation—and, sure, this *sounds* like juridical blood atonement or substitutionary-atonement-speak, but wait— *of all the pains that lead to salvation, this is the greatest: to see the lover suffer.* This is absolutely the key to understanding Julian, and absolutely key to making real sense out of the meaning of Tau. It is the key to understanding and feeling the wisdom of the cross.

According to Julian, the worst suffering imaginable is the greatest suffering, and the greatest suffering is the suffering that leads to salvation, and the suffering that leads to salvation is *to see the beloved suffer.* This is greater than any personally experienced pain. Julian is recognizing in herself the reality that she is empathetically suffering the suffering of Jesus, her beloved. In fact, *there is no pain that can be suffered like the sorrow she feels to see her beloved in pain.*

Stay with this. Divine love has to be at least as sophisticated as Julian's human love. So, here is the rub: in spite of all the gory focus on the physical suffering of Christ in the crucifixion, the observations—*of all the pains that lead to salvation, this is the greatest: to see the lover suffer, and there was no pain which could be suffered like the sorrow which I felt to see him in pain*—mean that Jesus' greatest suffering also cannot be his physical wounds. Make no mistake: Julian's telling leaves no room for wondering if the crucifixion is a real physical suffering—it is. However, if Julian's greatest

33. Ibid.
34. Ibid.

human suffering is not bodily suffering, but is rather to *see the suffering of her beloved,* then a bodily suffering certainly can't be Christ's greatest suffering either. The physical wounding of Christ cannot be the suffering that leads to salvation. The interpretive key to the sufferings of the Tau is this: Christ's greatest suffering must also be empathetically sharing his beloved's suffering. The kind of suffering that leads to salvation is Christ's, or God's, *empathetic love suffering.*

Starting small, this means first that Christ's greatest suffering, and the suffering that leads to salvation,[35] is *suffering the sorrow of seeing his beloved in pain*; it is witnessing the suffering of his beloved, Julian. But that is just the beginning, because real love *loves the other so much more than the self.* Christ's beloved in not only Julian. *Actually,* Christ "saw and he sorrowed for every man's sorrow, desolation and anguish, in his compassion and love."[36] It is not some law or some substitutionary atonement at work here. Love cannot be the abusive sky parent killing his Son to save humanity. And Christ's suffering that saves is not his physical woundings. Instead, Christ's salvific suffering is sharing empathetically the suffering of his beloved: seeing and sorrowing for *everyone's* sorrow, desolation, and anguish in his compassion and love.

Jesus' beloved is not just Julian. No. God's beloved is *everyone who will be saved.* It might be tempting to read that at first to mean *Christians* or *those in the church.* But that is too stunted, too trivial for divine empathetic love suffering. Christ's greatest suffering, the pain that leads to salvation, is the empathetic love suffering of the entire creation, *no exceptions.* And Julian agrees with "no exceptions":

> And in this he showed me something small, no bigger than a hazelnut, lying in the palm of my hand, as it seemed to me, and it was as round as a ball . . . I was amazed that it could last, for I thought that because of its littleness it would suddenly have fallen into nothing. And I was answered in my understanding: It lasts and always will, because God loves it; and thus everything has being through the love of God.[37]

Everything has being through the love of God—no exceptions! That little ball will *last and not fall into nothingness* because of God's love. It will not be

35. To be saved means to be made whole, to be healed from disconnection. Love heals. Love makes whole. Love reunifies what has been separated.

36. Julian of Norwich, *Showings*, 213.

37. Ibid., 183.

lost. It will be saved. She nearly weeps to see that God creates it, loves it, and protects it: "In this little thing I saw three properties. The first is that God made it, the second is that God loves it, the third is that God preserves it."[38] God is not some impotent abuser whose love is expressed in violence! God is the creator and the lover and the protector. This is not stingy love. This is not conditional love. This is not a miserly application of the pain that leads to salvation: real divinity is real divine love that loves without discrimination. That is the meaning of *Omnicaritas*. And that real love comes from exercising real power that is in full accord with love, the power perfected in weakness through sharing the suffering of the beloved world.

Tau wisdom is the deep and abiding experience of empathetic love suffering. And it is empathetic love that shares even suffering—in addition to sharing in the delight and joy. It is *that* deep love that saves. It is not an abusive divine parent whose unthwartable will requires the death of his beloved Son that saves. The God whose love is utterly complete, uncompromising, and unconditional is the God that saves. That Tau wisdom can remove divine truthiness from the Christian imagination. Tau wisdom subverts the dangerous wisdom and logic of violence. The truth of power perfected in weakness makes sense when we know the God whose love is really love—the God who is all love, Omnicaritas—without remainder, so that all *will in fact* be well. Thank you, Julian.

The Loving Power Perfected in Weakness Is the Way of the Christ

The Tau in Christianity reveals that the power of the divine love works by these many ways:

- the divine self-emptying or kenosis as the primary character of divine love-power

- the power perfected in weakness, vulnerability, and retreat, as in the infant life of Christ

- the power of non-imperialist letting be, as in Jesus' response to temptations

- the powerless power of the poor, the captives, the blind, the oppressed

38. Ibid.

- the last who are first without reversing roles of perpetrator and victim the crucifixion of Christ, the crucified God, the suffering God

- the resurrection of Christ that restores lives and heals relationships

- the empathetic suffering of the suffering of the beloved: powerful love that saves

It is in all these ways, and no doubt many more, that Christians encounter the true nature of divine power. It is the paradox of powerless power; persuasive, alluring, essential to the natural processes of reality, non-imperial; power that absorbs the joys of a joyous world and the sufferings of a suffering world in a perfect empathy of love. That is the Christian revelation of Tau. That is the Christian meaning of Tau. That is the Christian answer to the truthy riddle of love and power. That Christian gift to the world causes Whitehead to contemplate the exquisite but "brief Galilean vision of humility" that "flickered throughout the ages, uncertainly."[39]

Lifting up that brief, uncertain flickering of powerful humility-love is how Christians can help us leave behind divine truthiness. But, is Christianity alone with Buddhism in this uncertainly flickering minority report of the *power of mutual becoming* which is *power perfected in weakness*? So often, in a framework of divine truthiness, Christians have seen the Christ event as so utterly unique that it eclipses any other truth. But Christian Tau is not alone with Buddhist Tathata. The life, message, death, and resurrection of Christ, in short, what is nearest and dearest to Christian self-understanding, is not some aberration in the history of religions. The doctrine of divine love-power that can be inferred from Tau and the Omnicaritas, and the power of the Tathata of reality, are in fact richly analogous to another religion's doctrine of power. In fact, something similar to the doctrine of *power perfected in weakness* is also the beating heart of Taoism. So we now breathe the fresh air: new hope for new communion with new neighbors. So, let us now turn to the wisdom of Taoism, all the while allowing ourselves to be supported and buoyed by the healing waters of the wisdom of Buddhist Tathata (which, as we saw in chapters 4, 5, and 20 is a widespread wisdom echoed in many realms of thought) and Christian Tau, in which we already find ourselves safely afloat.

---

39. Whitehead, *Process and Reality*, 342.

Chapter 22

Taoist Power: Tao of Tathata-Tau-Tao

P erhaps it is important again to take a moment to breathe, and remind ourselves where we've been, how we got here, and what is at stake. We have found that the regime of divine truthiness has created untenable and dangerous incoherencies in theology (who is God?) and anthropology (what is humanity?). As we have seen, rigid, violent forms of power wind up making no sense when we apply them to empathetic love. In short, we have been saddled with incongruent doctrines of power and love. To overcome that situation, we are turning to three religions: Buddhism, Christianity, and now Taoism. From a Buddhist perspective the pain of life comes when one's life is not in accord with Tathata, the vast interdependent co-arising of all. From a Christian perspective the undeniable revelation of the meaning of divine power and love are both found in the Tau of Christ. But, now in this chapter, we are exploring yet a third religion for a doctrine of real power in full accord with real love. We are turning to look into a religious philosophy known as *Taoism*. The beauty of including Taoism in this discussion at this point is the fact that its primary text, known as the *Tao Te Ching*, is mainly concerned with describing power that makes real sense with the way things actually are. In fact, we have no further to go than the title, *Tao Te Ching*, to see that its ultimate concern is power, since it is often translated as *The Way and Its Power*. And the shorthand symbol for that will be Tao, which literally means "the Way."

Taoism can be for us another companion on the path to ending enslavement to divine truthiness. The Taoist approach to reality in its suchness reveals for us soothing truth that abides in head no less than heart; in brain no less than belly; in gray matter no less than gut. Buddhist Tathata and Christian Tau break bread as true companions with Tao.

Now, let's be very clear. Tathata, Tau, and Tao are not *the same*. They each reveal important specialized details about the truth of real power.

We should not be imperialists who erase real differences. Taoism is really something all its own. Tao is its *own* way—*and* it is a way among other ways. In this brush with Taoist thought it is possible to experience a delightful camaraderie. It is possible to recognize something enlightening in the observations of a fellow traveler whose vision is clear and whose aspiration is true. We all live our lives on this same marvelous planet, with many of the same basic limits, needs, and resources. We all inquire into meaning. So, let's not be surprised when someone else discovers a truth with a recognizable melody, even though the notes are not the same. But, let us not hastily and absolutely identify the truth we encounter in the other with our own truth. It is not "the same." But, maybe if we sing our truth and our companions sing theirs, we will behold a rich new harmony that supports our voices in the places where our truth seems shaky or absent; a rich new harmony that bolsters our companions and likewise bridges the rests and silences in their singing of their truth. We *can* do this. We *can* attend in the domain of the mindful heart with a reflective spirit.[1]

Divine Truthiness and the Loss of Tao

In Taoism—as in many forms of Buddhism—there is not talk about a *God*. That fact should banish immediately any imperialist impulse to call Taoist, Buddhist, and Christian philosophies "the same." But, with no God in Taoism, how can we begin to speak a recognizable language with the vocabulary of divine truthiness? After all, the *divine* in divine truthiness points to *God*, so how could there be anything similar in Taoism, which does not point to *God*? The key is not to search for sameness. Divine truthiness is the loss of integrity between what we assent to with our mind and what we feel to be true in our heart. Divine truthiness is a breakdown of humanity

---

1. You may, as we proceed, recognize in my descriptions a real enthusiasm for Taoism. And you may recognize in my approach something like childlike enjoyment. And I am truly a wondering child in my relation to Taoism. I hope this does not offend. But, the truth is Taoism is not my native setting, and the truth is I do approach it with a sense of wonder and enjoyment. Frankly, I hope the same can be said of my descriptions of Buddhism, which have already been scattered throughout this book. Like any child, I am no doubt bound to stumble a bit as I learn to walk on these other paths. But, I hope you will be willing to toddle along with me on this adventure. Finally, you will see presently that I am profoundly indebted both to Alan Watts and Benjamin Hoff for their lovely and loving interpretations of Taoism for a Western audience—for someone like me.

by a process of dehumanization that requires the marginalization of half of what makes us human.

Taoism likewise recognizes that something has gone terribly wrong. The great Tao is the Way of All. The great Tao is the simple reality of all that mutually becomes. And the great Tao is beyond words, images, concepts, and philosophies. To begin the process of verbalizing, imaging, conceptualizing, and philosophizing about the great Tao means to run the great risk of believing we have captured the great Tao in our words, images, concepts, and philosophies.[2]

Taoism complains about the human tendency to introduce false complexity, in the forms of words, images, concepts, philosophies, categories, distinctions, measurements, judgments, etc., to the simple fact of *reality as it becomes* (think, something akin to Tathata). Thought seems to require it. Taoism looks back to a primordial past when humans lost touch with the great Tao. In Alan Watts's translation of the *Tao Te Ching* the loss is described this way: "When the great Tao was lost, there came (ideas of) humanity and justice. When knowledge and cleverness arrived, there came deceptions. When familial relations went out of harmony, there came (ideas of) good parents and loyal children. When the nation fell into disorder and misrule, there came (ideas of) loyal ministers."[3] Taoism counsels vigilance for the *deceptions* or the *hypocrisy* that accompany *knowledge and cleverness*. The workings of human heads, human minds, human intelligences often put people at odds with the great Tao, which governs metaphorical human hearts. My literal heart in my chest beats whether or not I describe it, categorize it, and understand it with ideas and concepts. There is a sense in Taoism that the boys from Liverpool were on to something when they counseled us to *let things be*. And people need that counsel because we have lost the great Tao: we *don't* let things be, and we need to be reminded. To sum up, *divine truthiness* has a familiar resonance with the Taoist complaint about the *loss of the great Tao*. Both point toward recognizing the tragedy of that violent separation of head and heart, in tragic opposition to genuine powerful love as the integrated wholeness we can call *holiness*.

---

2. It is worth noting that many God-traditions largely will admit similar things about God: God is likewise beyond all words, images, concepts, and philosophies. And to begin the process of verbalizing, imaging, conceptualizing, and philosophizing about God also runs the great risk that we will believe we have captured God in our words, images, concepts, and philosophies. This is not to say that the Tao is the same thing as God.

3. Watts and Huang, *Tao: The Watercourse Way*, 112.

Of course Tao is beyond even the most apt and best expressions. But, if we are going to say anything reliable about Tao (or divinity, or Tathata, or God, for that matter), the only source of all our symbols and words is the actual world around us. So every expression and symbol we use requires at least a basic framework for the analogy between the universe and its supreme source.[4] The *Tao Te Ching* shares a deep wisdom to understand the continuity from ultimate reality to everyday existence: "The world had a beginning And in this beginning could be the mother of the world. When you know the mother Go on to know the child. After you have known the child Go back to holding fast to the mother."[5] In other words, careful observation of the actual world makes it possible to know something about its source, Tao. In chapter 25 of the *Tao Te Ching*, Lao Tzu, the author, describes this *principle of continuity* in this way: "Man models himself on earth, Earth on heaven, Heaven on the way, And the way on that which is naturally so."[6] This is a description of the *chain of continuity*. Like gives rise to like. So, each little existence is a further unfolding of the origination of existence itself. It is a manifestation of Tao. And in that chain of continuity resides hope to make sense and meaning of life by connecting what is encounterable in the here and now with its ineffable divine or ultimate source.

Human beings are intricately woven into the chain of continuity—embedded in Tao. That means both of the following things are true: 1) the Great Tao is beyond our capacity to theorize and categorize; and 2) it is as intimately close to us as anything can ever be. In this spirit, Alan Watts challenges:

> if, as is the case, the Tao is simply inconceivable, what is the use of having the word and of saying anything at all about it? Simply because we know intuitively that there is a dimension of ourselves and of nature which eludes us and too all embracing to be singled out because it is too close, too general, to be singled out as a particular object. This dimension is the ground of all the astonishing forms and experiences of which we are aware.[7]

---

4. And, a Christian may recognize a Gospel parallel when Matthew 7:16 gives the principle, "You will know them by their fruits," which applies here: people can know something about the God who is the source of creation by knowing the "fruit," that is, by knowing the creation.

5. Lao Tzu, *Tao Te Ching*, 59.

6. Ibid., 30.

7. Watts and Huang, *Tao: The Watercourse Way*, 55.

Because the search for meaning is worth doing, we cannot merely be shut down by the impossibility of saying a final word about the Tao. Just because we cannot say the final word does not mean we cannot say the first word, or the intermediate word, the words *in-munu*—the middle of existence (see chapter 14). We speak each word so we can move toward a reunification (atonement) of heart and mind. People deserve the chance to live as whole beings with harmonious hearts and minds in accord with Tao. After all, the idols of truthiness are false gods of our own creation that are undeserving of our allegiance, anyway.

The great Tao abides in everything, so the great Tao abides in human beings whether they know it or not, whether they can say it or not. Adequate articulation is not a prerequisite for knowing or feeling that truths really are true. But wouldn't it be great to know it, feel it, and to be able to say it too? Remember, to find Tao we only have to touch the world, because the world comes from Tao, and it is Tao. But, we must be ever on guard against the influences of divine truthiness, the influences that seem so coercive that they further enforce a regime of false separation from the great Tao.

Tao and Love

As is no doubt obvious, Christianity is my native soil. So, when I encounter other religions I am always on the lookout for inklings of love. In a way, the Christian question of interreligious encounter is always, *is this love?* So, a Christian love orientation (the empathetic love of Omnicaritas) might leap to attention upon reading in the *Tao Te Ching* that "the sage does not hoard. Having bestowed all he has on others, he has yet more; Having given all he has to others, he is richer still"[8] Much as in the chapter 22 conversation about the Tau, here we learn that the practitioner of Tao flourishes by the principle of generosity. Surely this kind of limitless generosity has *some*thing to do with empathetic love (see chapters 6–9).

Martin Aronson's "parallel sayings" between Lao Tzu and Jesus further perk these hopes as he proposes there is rich congruency in the Gospel injunction, "Be children of your Father in heaven; for he makes his sun rise on the evil and on the good, and sends rain on the righteous and on the unrighteous" (Matt 5:45)[9] with the Taoist saying, "Heaven and earth enjoying the sweet rain falls beyond the command of people yet evenly upon all" (*Tao*

8. Lao Tzu, *Tao Te Ching*, 88.

9. Aronson, *Jesus and Lao Tzu*, 80.

Te Ching 32).[10] Supreme generosity rains down on all, whether they meet human criteria for "worthiness" or not. The wisdom of Tao, seemingly much in accord with the wisdom of Tau, transgresses the truthy rigid notions of calculated justice and the categories of deserving and undeserving. The great Tao, the source of all, gives to all. Sounds a lot like love.

Alan Watts expands for us the terrain of Taoist love by recounting the words of the great Chuang Tzu (a second founder of Taoism): "They love one another without being conscious of charity. They are true without being conscious of loyalty. They are honest without being conscious of good faith. They act freely in all things without recognizing obligations to anyone. Thus, their deeds leave no trace . . . "[11] Yes! Real love does not squander energy to name, categorize, describe, and account for its activities.

We can delight in familiarity when we hear on the one hand Jesus say, "Love your neighbor as yourself" (Matt 22:39), and on the other hand Lao Tzu say, "Love the world as your own self" (*Tao Te Ching* 13).[12] Confident in a starting point of rather compatible—though not literally "the same"—notions of love makes it possible to move to the heart of the issue. Does Taoism present a doctrine of ultimate power that is compatible with authentic ultimate love, which I am calling Omnicaritas?

Water Power.
Noncontention Is the Taoist Way of Saying Non-Coercion

The beautiful truth is that in Taoism we do meet with power that is compatible with love. At the very heart of Taoism is the whole notion of noncontention. And a failure to understand this Taoist way of non-contentious, powerless power would be a complete failure to understand Tao. By and large in Christianity, and in the West in general, it seems like a bizarre Zen koan that the power of God is demonstrated in the powerlessness of the Tau. But, in Taoism powerless power is basically presupposed. Taoists might say, *of course powerless power is Tao!*

The Platonic discovery—that persuasion is ultimately a more effective force in the universe than coercion—finds a traveling companion in Taoism, which is also ultimately concerned with the manner of the working of the universe. The ongoing self-creation of the world has a certain

---

10. Ibid., 81.

11. Watts and Huang, *Tao: The Watercourse Way*, 80.

12. Aronson, *Jesus and Lao Tzu*, 74–75.

character that endures. That enduring character is not rigidity and hardness and force. The enduring character is non-contentious Tao power, which is more pliant, perhaps softer, ultimate power.

In Taoism, the finest symbol of that pliant, non-contentious, ultimate power is *water*. According to the *Tao Te Ching*, "Highest good is like water."[13] In fact, Alan Watts even decides to name his book on Taoism *The Watercourse Way*. With that title he tries to express to a Western audience the common sense in Taoism that real power is like the power exerted by water. The *Tao Te Ching* teaches, "because water excels in benefiting the myriad creatures without contending with them and settles where none would like to be, it comes close to the way."[14] It comes close to Tao. Water does not insist on having its own way immediately. Water settles in, absorbs, dissolves, and moves, thereby overcoming the most rigid, the supposedly strongest of rock and mountain. Whereas the common notion might be that a rock is "strong," Taoism recognizes the real power: power exemplified by water, power that does not contend.

There is a divine truthiness that infests notions of ultimate force. The *Tao Te Ching* is every bit as much a manual to unteach divine truthiness as is Christian Tau or Buddhist Tathata. Please call to mind what has already been said about the coercion of the truthy Omnipotent God, the God who has all the power and enforces his will. That kind of coercion diminishes anything we might think of as God into a puny enforcer of violence. Aronson recognizes that both Christianity and Taoism see violence as "a deadly form of hypocrisy" and "both Jesus and Lao Tzu wearily denounce it as humankind's most regrettable vice."[15] How tragic and ironic it would be for us to elevate humankind's most regrettable vice to the status of divinity, or the status of ultimate meaning! To do that is precisely the occupation of the regime of divine truthiness.

If we think that Tao at its heart is violent, then what is to stop us from responding to the urge to be "like" that violent way? An analogue to the image-imitation dynamic is very much at work here: if a person knows she is composed of Tao, then she may wish to conform herself to Tao as best she knows it. This can be holy if our view is wholesome, and it can be disintegrating if our view is unwholesome. Lao Tzu teaches, "A violent man will die a violent death" (*Tao Te Ching* 42); likewise, Christ teaches, "All who take

13. Lao Tzu, *Tao Te Ching*, 12.

14. Ibid.

15. Aronson, *Jesus and Lao Tzu*, 111.

the sword will perish by the sword. (Matt 26:25).[16] Lao Tzu and Jesus hand on these teachings precisely because they need to be taught. The truth has been forgotten. The great Tao is lost because divine truthiness is blinding and deafening.

Wu Wei: Overcoming by Yielding

One of the Taoist principles that we can use to understand this water-like, non-violent, non-contending power is called *wu wei*. Another popular interpreter of Taoism for Westerners, Benjamin Hoff, thinks that a good way to understand *wu wei* is to look at the martial art *tai chi*, "the basic idea of which is to wear an opponent out either by sending his energy back at him or by deflecting it away, in order to weaken his power, balance, and position-for-defense."[17] The strongest man cannot to beat up the ocean with his fists. Or better yet, "never is force opposed with force; instead it is overcome with yielding."[18] The strongest man who has fallen overboard into the ocean cannot succeed in staying alive by going rigid or by exerting muscular force: these are the most certain means by which that strong man will drown. Only yielding, softness, and participation in the water's flow and motion will preserve the strong man's life. Hoff uses the example of a cork floating in water to demonstrate the meaning of *wu wei*. He says, "the harder you hit it, the more it yields; the more it yields, the harder it bounces back. Without expending energy, the cork can easily wear you out. So, *wu wei* overcomes force by neutralizing its power, rather than by adding to the conflict."[19] This is such a window into the truth of reality. It doesn't matter how strong you think you are. The cork will win. And it will win without trying, without contending. In fact the only reason you "lose" is through the very act of contention.[20] That is the meaning of *wu wei*—the power that yields (you may wish to call to mind Tau power, which *gives in*, *gives way*, and *gives all*).

---

16. Ibid., 120–21.

17. Hoff, *Tao of Pooh*, 87.

18. Ibid.

19. Ibid., 88.

20. Of course, I am mindful of the soft irony that I am attempting to persuade you by laying out my various contentions about the truth of how things really are—who I think God is and what I think is meant by Tao—in the hopes that you might agree with me.

No Self-Violence Either

An easy mistake to make here is to think that a regime of force should be replaced by a regime of enforced calmness. Do we think we can insist on non-contention? Alan Watts rightly says, "Taoism is not a philosophy of compelling oneself to be calm and dignified under all circumstances."[21] The power described here should be no less violent against oneself than it is outwardly. In fact, in a way, the person who is violent to herself in the quiet of her thoughts is doing nothing more than rehearsing the ways in which she will be well-versed in enacting violence against someone else out there, in the world. Martin Luther famously talks about the self-inflicted violence we do in the effort to abide by commands. To illustrate his point Luther appeals to the example of "the commandment, 'You shall not covet' [Exod. 20:17], [which] is a command which proves us all to be sinners, for no one can avoid coveting no matter how much he may struggle against it."[22] Don't believe it? What does the one who strives do with the fact that he *covets the state of not coveting*? Contending is a spiral of self-inflicted violence. Was Luther Taoist?

But, it is not only religion that contains these sorts of truthy imperatives to self-violent behavior. Watts calls to mind how

> in many cultures people are brought up to mistrust their own organisms, and, as children, are taught to control their thoughts, emotions, and appetites by muscular efforts such as clenching the teeth or fists, frowning to concentrate attention, scratching the head to think, staring to see, holding the breath or tightening the diaphragm or rectum to inhibit emotion.[23]

These are not isolated examples. Taoism teaches that these insidious self-violences, and the violences that explode out against others, are absurd in the extreme. Do we think that contentious power, power over against, is the way real accomplishments are achieved? Do we think it is appropriate to "use a sledgehammer for tuning a radio"?[24] If we do, we are mistaken. To be coerced into that kind of confusion means to be bereft of intelligence,[25] to be duped into believing mere violent or insistent force can accomplish

---

21. Watts and Huang, *Tao: The Watercourse Way*, 122.

22. Luther, *On Christian Liberty*, 11–12.

23. Watts and Huang, *Tao: The Watercourse Way*, 118.

24. Ibid.

25. This is just the sort of dehumanizing garbage that animates divine truthiness, after all.

anything wholesome. Watts brilliantly illustrates this absurdity. He paints the picture of "a cigar-chewing Texan who harnessed a kitten to his broken-down Cadillac. When bystanders pointed out that this was absurd, he replied, 'You-all may think so, but I got a horsewhip.'"[26] Funny, right? Humor is good because it can gently loosen the grip of divine truthiness. There is a humanizing moment when head and heart are allowed to commune without contention, without banishing one or the other. The way of Taoists (and recall, *way* is Tao) contains "no designs to subjugate or alter the universe by force or willpower, for their art is entirely to go along with the flow of things in an intelligent way."[27] That is the watercourse way: it is the weight of physicality and the direction of intelligence mutually oriented and healthful. The authentic power of the universe is the non-contentious and non-coercive power of water; the *wu wei* power that yields; the power that does no violence to itself; and the power that does not export violence to others. In short, this is the wisdom of Tao.

Tao Power: The Way and Its Power

The wisdom way of the *Tao Te Ching* presents coherent and satisfying approaches to power inherent in reality from Alpha through MUNU right up to Omega. But, the influence of the regime of divine truthiness is relevant in the imagination world from which Taoism springs, every bit as much as it is relevant in the imagination world from which Christianity and Buddhism spring. Lao Tzu warns against the weakness of worldly wisdom, speaking almost in paradoxical riddles, much as does the Apostle Paul. For instance, in the *Tao Te Ching* 81 Lao Tzu says, "the wise one does not know many things; one who knows many things is not wise."[28] In fact we are even counseled to "banish 'wisdom' and discard 'knowledge'" because this will make people "hundred times happier."[29] This cannot mean that authentic wisdom and authentic knowledge are anathema. What it must mean is that it is so common to misunderstand, so common to be influenced by wrong sorts of wisdom and knowledge (à la divine truthiness), that if they are the only likely outcome it is better to declare them all out of bounds.

---

26. Watts and Huang, *Tao: The Watercourse Way*, 119.

27. Ibid., 90.

28. Aronson, *Jesus and Lao Tzu*, 15.

29. Ibid., 17., *Tao Te Ching* 19.

This might be reminiscent of the times in Mark's Gospel when Jesus tells people not to spill the beans that he is the Messiah. He says not to say he is Messiah because people have wrong ideas of what the word *Messiah* means. It is a calculated cost-benefit analysis: Jesus knows if you say *Messiah* the people will have in their mind notions of military and political overpowering power. The problem, from Jesus' view, is that he offers precisely the opposite of that kind of power. Likewise, Lao Tzu knows that the authentic wisdom of Tao is the way of liberation, but he also knows there is great risk in misunderstanding. Similarly, while Jesus knows that the brand of power he has to offer is the way of liberation, he also knows there is great risk in misunderstanding. Words matter. How we define them matters.

Here is how Chuang Tzu expresses that conundrum: "A well-frog cannot imagine the ocean, nor can a summer insect conceive of ice. How then can a scholar understand the Tao? He is restricted by his own learning."[30] We are well-frogs who cannot understand the ocean. We are summer insects who cannot understand ice. We are human beings so conditioned by tragic notions of divine truthiness, *the loss of the great Tao*, that oddly enough it is the *truth* that seems to be outlandish or impossible.

It is a little ironic to mention this in a book, but the problem might be people like academics, scholars, and writers. Benjamin Hoff muses, "it seems rather odd, somehow, that Taoism, the way of the Whole Man, the True Man, the Spirit Man (to use a few Taoist terms), is for the most part interpreted here in the West by the Scholarly . . . by the Brain, the Academician, the dry-as-dust Absentminded Professor."[31] That might be a little harsh, but he gets his meaning across. We should never dehumanize ourselves by either ignoring our head or disregarding our heart because an expert tells us that's how to find the truth.

Make no mistake. This is tricky business. I am a participant in the human endeavor to categorize and make sense of the vast complexity of which my experience is only one tiny part. Of course I have to believe that trying to harmonize my head and my heart is a useful enterprise. I have to believe it is worthwhile to write a book and challenge all of us to live with authentic feeling and thinking. Hoff talks about this as the common practice of organization by "the following of linear rules and laws imposed from above—that is, of strung-out, serial, one-thing-at–at-a-time sequences of

30. Hoff, *Tao of Pooh*, 24.
31. Ibid., 25.

words and signs which can never grasp the complexity of nature."[32] But that is the nature of words: one-at-a-time sequencing. Maybe I should be painting this, or humming it, or dancing it. But then I have to consider that my brain and my intellect are no less a part of everything than the colors that come off the edge of a paintbrush, or the hum that expresses through buzzing lips, or the choreography of lithe limbs. Is our true nature, our true calling, to be thinkers, painters, singers, and dancers? Probably. I am writing this. Will you paint it? Will you sing it? Will you dance it? I hope so. But this is a book, so here comes the next sequential word . . .

What Hoff is getting at is the problem of *confusing the map for the terrain*, as they say. The minute people allow themselves to think their categories and notions are the truth itself, is the moment they lose the possibility of actually encountering the truth itself. He points out that "nature is only 'complex' in relation to the impossible task of translating it into these linear signs."[33] Actually, there is a serene simplicity in Tao—the sheer Tathata of the mutual becoming of all beings.

Not only should we not confuse the map with the terrain, we should not allow the map to confuse us. Sure, there are trillions of interrelationships that make your fingers possible—and it is beyond your conscious mind's capacity to understand or control those interrelations. But you don't have to despair over that. Instead, you can just use your hands! Instead, you can be grateful for your hands. Instead you can be generous with your hands. In other words, you can just let them be hands. That is Tao wisdom.

The danger with stunted linear thought is that it implies power as power-over-against, because it implies hierarchy by the mere fact of sequencing. Something has to come first, something second, something third. And depending on the perspective, that first thing might seem best, or that third thing might seem best, etc. But to be mindful and heartful that hierarchies and sequences are meant only to point towards the truth, and that they don't replace the truth, makes it possible to breathe in the real truth of Tao that "the way of heaven excels in overcoming though it does not contend."[34]

That is a wide-eyed and full-throated reversal of worldly wisdom. This reversal of worldly wisdom is the wisdom of Tao. It is the watercourse way that everyone has seen in action. This is the reversal of worldly wisdom that takes as its main evidence the world itself, *as it is*, because "in the world

32. Ibid., 44.
33. Ibid.
34. Lao Tzu, *Tao Te Ching*, 80.

there is nothing more submissive and weak than water. Yet for attacking that which is hard and strong nothing can surpass it. This is because there is nothing that can take its place."[35] Nothing can take the place of the submissive and the weak.

What Everyone Knows, but No One Can Do?

The coercive idiocy of divine truthiness has reigned too long. And there is one particularly exasperated and beautiful statement in the *Tao Te Ching* that expresses this best of all: "That the weak overcomes the strong, And the submissive overcomes the hard, Everyone in the world knows yet no one can put this knowledge into practice."[36] Marvelous! Everyone knows it, but no one can do it! But is that really so? Of course, most human-developed structures assume that the *hard overcomes the submissive*. It is the wisdom traditions, embodied in Tathata-Tau-Tao, that are certain that the opposite is really the truth. And maybe we really do know it too when we think back over the long-term of our experiences. *Everyone seems to know this is true but no one seems to be able to employ this wisdom as a first strategy*. And it is precisely at this point that a bright and thoughtful Christian might wrinkle her nose and say, *wait a second—maybe Jesus did it?* Maybe he did. Maybe it's just that sort of thing that made some of his followers come to the conclusion that in his life the divinity was made incarnate, made to be in the flesh, and put into action. But, the doctrine of the incarnation can have the effect of absolving us of the responsibility to act likewise: after all I'm no God, so how can I be expected to act like God? But, what if Jesus' example is a *call to actually do it*—in the best imitation of Christ, the best imitation of God? And imagine what it means that the *Tao Te Ching* is calling for something so similar. Imagine that. After all, *everyone in the world knows that the submissive overcomes the hard. Everyone knows that power is peaceable, gentle, compliant, and merciful. Can we finally live Tao, the Tathata of Tau power made perfect in weakness*?

And, can we imagine that it wasn't a bizarre anomaly that Jesus was able to *put into practice what everyone knows is true*, that *the submissive overcomes the hard*, but rather Jesus' life was just the incarnation of the divine power and love that a Taoist would recognize as Tao? The Christ event only *seems* like a bizarre anomaly because of the trap of the regime of divine truthiness.

35. Ibid., 85.
36. Ibid.

Actually, Tau effortlessly points to the truth that "softness and gentleness are the companions of life. The hard and strong will fall. The soft and weak will overcome,"[37] which are Taoist words, not Christian ones. And that means to say the wisdom of the world is reversed not by appealing to an otherworldly wisdom, but by appealing to the truth we already somehow know, and appealing for the courage to faithfully put it into practice.

Wisdom Incarnate:
Tao Is Living According to How Things Are

There is an early Christian idea that predates talk of Jesus as Word (*Logos*) incarnate, that Jesus Christ was Wisdom (*Sophia*) incarnate. The cross exemplifies the incarnation of Wisdom: Tau wisdom is wisdom made flesh and put into action. Those early Christians proposed that the wise Word of God is incarnate in the words, deeds, and Tau of Christ. That Christian basic self-understanding appears to be an answer to that insightful observation of the *Tao Te Ching*: "That the weak overcomes the strong, And the submissive overcomes the hard, Everyone in the world knows yet no one can put this knowledge into practice."[38] But, Lao Tzu isn't really confounded. The truth is, he sees the enfleshment, embodiment, enactment of Tao literally everywhere. It is a peculiarly truthy human dilemma to be separated from the living out of Tao. Left to their natural tendencies, the ordinary mutual unfolding of all beings just happens. For a Taoist, it is not a matter of looking in one and only one place to see the highest principle enacted and enfleshed. One need only look everywhere. The non-contention of *wu wei* melts away the separatedness of head and heart, and gives way to what Watts astutely calls "the 'unconscious' intelligence of the whole organism."[39]

That phrase, *the unconscious intelligence of the whole organism*, is such a sweet way of harmonizing the feeling of the heart with the knowing of the head, and thereby banishing divine truthiness. Watts goes on to say that "Wu-wei is a combination of this wisdom [of innate unconscious intelligence] with taking the line of least resistance in all one's actions. It is not the mere avoidance of effort."[40] The power that does not contend is not the power that does not do. Hoff explains that "*Wu Wei* [means] 'Do Without

---

37. Aronson, *Jesus and Lao Tzu*, 65; Lao Tzu, *Tao Te Ching*, 76.

38. Lao Tzu, *Tao Te Ching*.

39. Watts and Huang, *Tao: The Watercourse Way*, 76.

40. Ibid.

Doing."[41] Doing happens. But it does not require me to *do*. Perhaps that is still mystifying, but this might help: "When you work with Wu Wei, you put the round peg in a round hole and the square peg in a square hole. No stress, no struggle."[42] The doing is non-contentious when the pegs and the holes participate in one another. Things fit. No exertion of faulty, excessive, or coercive power is required. Imperialism and omnipotence need not apply.

Yet, the regime of separatedness, of truthiness, wages a compelling force against us, and so we strive to make fit those things which do not fit. We exert our energies to demand the square peg inhabit the round hole. And when our imposed rule of enforced law is not followed we fear anarchy's encroachment. Watts rightly observes, "our human fear is that the Tao which cannot be described, the order which cannot be put into books, is chaos."[43] And even if we escape those fears, we are accustomed to resorting to another mistaken notion. We must not fall into the trap of thinking that the *Way* and its *power* are of the character of an imposed law. Rather, the left-alone Way (let-it-be nature) of things discloses itself as natural. There is nothing that is not the embodiment of Tao. Or more positively, everything is an incarnation of Tao.

Tao incarnates itself in each and every one of the countless instances "that things happen by themselves, spontaneously."[44] This principle has the name *tzu-jan*, which means literally "self so,"[45] or perhaps better, the free self-happening-ness of any being. And we have access to the sublime reality of the free self-happening nature of beings. The confounding thing is that here, in a book, words are required to describe that self-happening nature, that *tzu-jan*, in terms of a process of mutual becoming that can be experienced—consciously with the mind, unconsciously with feelings—but cannot really be depicted in words.

Human beings are not exceptions to Tao, and its free self-happening-nature. Human beings are further exemplifications of it. Human beings are creatures of an entire universe that unfolds, as like from like, from a divine source, according to the Tathata of the Tao. The breathtaking continuity extends, according to Whitehead, even to *God, who is the chief exemplification,*

41. Hoff, *Tao of Pooh*, 70.

42. Ibid., 75.

43. Watts and Huang, *Tao: The Watercourse Way*, 44.

44. Hoff, *Tao of Pooh*, 70.

45. Ibid.

not the chief exemption, for all we know of reality.[46] Watts finds that sort of continuity in Taoism, when he rightly observes that we may "pick up a blade of grass and all the worlds come with it. In other words, the whole cosmos is implicit in every member of it, and every point in it may be regarded as its center. This is the bare and basic principle of the organic view . . ."[47] Of course, in Taoism, that doesn't mean some divine being, some god, is reflected in each of the countless creatures. Rather, each creature is a particular expression of the general truths out of which its being is made possible. Each in its own manner reflects Tao.

So, what does it mean to *embody Tao*? It means that we are what we are composed of. It means to be what one is in one's *intrinsic nature*. To illustrate the notion of *intrinsic nature*, Watts quotes Chuang Tzu:

> Those who cannot make perfect without arc, line, compasses, and square, injure the natural constitution of things. Those who require cords to bind and glue to stick, interfere with the natural functions of things. And those who seek to satisfy the mind of man by fussing with ceremonies and music and preaching charity and duty to one's neighbor, thereby destroy the intrinsic nature of things. For there is such an intrinsic nature of things, in this sense:—Things which are curved require no arcs; things which are straight require no lines; things which are round require no compasses; things which are rectangular require no squares; things which stick require no glue; things which hold together require no cords.[48]

The *tzu-jan*, which is the free, unforced self-happening-ness of creatures, needs to be encountered, acknowledged, and respected. When round is allowed to be round, and square to be square, and smooth to be smooth, and rough to be rough (and stone is allowed to be stone!) we may be surprised to encounter a functional harmony among the diversity that we in our wiser moments can acknowledge as superior to human-imposed symmetry, repetition, and regimentation. Can we respect that? And can we respect it without degenerating into a mindless or heartless sort of libertarianism that elevates the good of the individual over against the organic mutuality? I *feel* we can. I *think* we can.

---

46. Whitehead, *Process and Reality*, 343.

47. Watts and Huang, *Tao: The Watercourse Way*, 35.

48. Ibid., 110.

Hsian Sheng, Mutual Becoming, and Tathata

That kind of respect is possible when we take even a moment to soak in the question of what makes this moment possible. The fact is that the present moment is composed of a massive contribution from the entire span of the previous universe. In other words, all that manifests right now is a spectacular gift from everything that preceded it.

The manner in which the *Tao Te Ching* describes the Way and how to participate in the Way's process is instructive: "The way is empty, yet use will not drain it. Deep, it is like the ancestor of the myriad creatures. Blunt the sharpness; Untangle the knots; Soften the glare; Let your wheels move only along old ruts."[49] The donation of Tao, the Way, to the present is an undrainable abundance. And, the *old ruts* show the safe way to pass into an authentically new, free self-happening now. There is a powerful and gentle assurance that comes from the vast interrelationality of the whole cosmic precedence—and this assurance is a simple *All*. It is a *universe*. And we are members of that *All*, members of that *universe*, inheritors of its assurances, and the standard bearers of its risks and rewards. All of that is gifted to us *and* we are not in charge of it. *Hallelujah!* that I am not in charge. My human expectations of symmetry, repetition, and regimentation, of categorization and systemization, simply do not apply to the self-happening nature of anything. I cannot even fathom, let alone take responsibility for, the multitude of interrelational events that conspire in an unimaginable symphony whose music is the working of my pinky finger. Walt Whitman says it better: "the narrowest hinge in my hand puts to scorn all machinery . . . And a mouse is miracle enough to stagger sextillions of infidels."[50] I stagger toward fidelity.

The Taoist understanding of reality *as it is* in its *true nature* is described by the term *hsian sheng*, which is the Taoist idea that emerged in an ancient dialogue with Buddhism's interdependent co-arising of all phenomena. *Hsian sheng* is the observation that all things arise mutually—and nothing can be separated from any other thing. So, Taoists no less than Buddhists recognize that "because of the mutual interdependence of all beings, they will harmonize if left alone and not forced into conformity with some arbitrary, artificial, and abstracts notion of order, and this harmony will emerge *tzu-jan*, of itself, without external compulsion."[51]

49. Lao Tzu, *Tao Te Ching*, 8.
50. Whitman, *Leaves of Grass*, 57.
51. Watts and Huang, *Tao: The Watercourse Way*.

This mutual becoming (Taoist *hsian sheng*, Buddhist *pratitya-samutpada*) is the means by which all power is expressed in all beings: it is the Tathata of reality. This power of mutual becoming is illustrated in Taoism again by the excellent metaphor of water, and is not altogether unlike the Christian metaphor of kenosis, the self-emptying love that also works by the power of mutual becoming. And this power is already present even in the title of the *Tao Te Ching* as the *te*. According to Benjamin Hoff, "In classical Chinese, [*te*] is written two ways. The first joins the characters for 'upright' to the character for 'heart.' Its meaning is virtue. The second way as the character for 'left foot,' which in Chinese signifies 'stepping out.' Its meaning is *virtue in action*."[52] Note that it does *not* mean virtue as *opposed to vice*. Rather, it is "a quality of special character, spiritual strength, or hidden potential unique to the individual—something that comes from the Inner Nature of things;"[53] and that phrase, *the inner nature of things*, could be an excellent definition of Tathata. That makes sense because we have just seen that the gift of the inner nature of things is the fact of its power of mutual becoming, or *hsian sheng*. No thing is what it is apart from its relation to every other thing. Mutuality of becoming is the governing power making free self-happening (*tzu-jan*) possible. In other words, *te* is the vast potency donated to every being by every other being. *Te* is the vital power that steps out, becomes something new. *Te* is the vital power that empties itself in kenosis that makes possible *each fresh mutual becoming*. The interrelations that mutually compose all beings are so perfectly ordinary that they are the very water the fish breathes, the very air the human breathes. Mutual becoming is so universally ordinary that it goes mostly undetected. Failing to appreciate mutual becoming can be such a tragedy. When we miss the truth of Tathata we misunderstand Tao and waste our time obsessing about what divides us, rather than rejoicing in the rich solidarity of fellowship in creation.

52. Hoff, *Te of Piglet*, 22.
53. Ibid.

Chapter 23

Tathata-Tau-Tao is the Power of Love

The genuine power at the furthest foundation and in the stepping out of *every* being is one and the same power—a power made perfect in weakness. It is the power that is self-emptying kenosis, crucifixion, yielding, non-violence, weakness, vulnerability, retreat, non-coercion, non-contention, non-imperialism. It is the power of the captive, the blind, the oppressed. It is the power of sympathetic love suffering. It is the power of solidarity. It is the power of mutual becoming.

As is no doubt clear by now, my primary worry stone is making sense of love with power that does not turn love into perversions like violence and hatred. And my answer is to point us in the direction of these three religious ways of wisdom: Tathata wisdom, Tau wisdom, and Tao wisdom. I have argued that the three wisdoms of *power made perfect in weakness* are only a riddle because of the enforcement of regimes of divine truthiness that violently dehumanize us by divorcing our head from our heart. All we need is to step out into freedom to be liberated from our enshacklement to incoherent and dangerous doctrines of power that make a mockery of the sway of our hearts toward love, and the inclining of our minds towards that same love. The revealing of *what we already all know, but somehow fail to apply* is that real power gives way; is submission and weakness that overcomes strength; is peaceable, gentle, compliant, and merciful. And that is the kind of power necessary for authentic love. When we understand power in this way, then love is allowed to be love. That's the meaning of Omnicaritas. And the truthy riddle is removed.

We are now equipped to see unified love and power that delight us as a unification of head and heart. We know love and power rooted in Tathata, rooted in Tau, rooted in Tao; love and power that honor our rational minds; love and power that appeal to our tender hearts. The power that is consistent with divine love is the power of mutual becoming, the Tathata of reality taught by the Buddha. The power that is consistent with divine love is the power perfected in weakness, the Tau of Christ. The power that is consistent with divine love is the submissive, weak, non-contentious water-power that overcomes the strong, known as Tao. We all know that Tathata-Tau-Tao power is true. Now it's time to put it into action.

Part 5

Ending Divine Truthiness

God's infinite power does not lead us to flee his fatherly tenderness, because in him affection and strength are joined. Indeed, all sound spirituality entails both welcoming divine love and adoration, confident in the Lord because of his infinite power.[1]

POPE FRANCIS

D ivine truthiness, with all its wrongheaded and wronghearted theologies, is the perpetrator of many injustices. Wrong theologies are translated into dangerous real-life situations by their conflation with the idea that humans are created in the image and likeness of that horrible, false, and downright truthy God. Who is the truthy God we too often imitate? Here's a quick recap:

If we have a God who is the *Imperial Ruler*, we think the human calling is to be a tyrant who imposes empire. If we have a God who is the *Absolute Moralist*, then the meaning of non-human creation is erased since it is not governed by morality, and worse, the shackles the tyrants decide to put on us seem to be given the divine blessing. If we have a God who is the *statically perfect Unmoved Mover*, exempt from change of any kind, then we are left devaluing creation, which is dynamically "imperfect," which can be a divine permission for the objectification and destruction of creatures and persons. Closely related to that, when we have the God who is the *Supreme Owner*, we think that the people who are owners are the ones who enact and properly

---

1.Pope Francis, *Laudato Si'*, 53.

reflect the divine image, while impoverished people are somehow less godlike. When God's simple oneness is worshipped as an idol, in the *Cult of Onlyness*, as the impossible goal of hopelessly complex and changeable creatures, that idolatry devalues a pluralistic world. If we have a God who is *Literally Male*, then we elevate the male human and devalue the female human because she fails to provide a reliable reflection of that male deity. When we submit to the temptations of "literal interpretation" of the Bible, we turn ourselves into mini-gods who are infallible in our interpretations and expressions. When we have a God who is *omnipotent*, then the causes and conditions and laws of this reality are ruined, and are made into the playthings of a capricious God who intervenes on behalf of some and imposes horrific sufferings and death on others. In fact, that leads to a divine love expressed as violent, authoritarian power-over creatures—which reveals the puniest kind of God, the God with all the power who enforces his will on those who by definition have no power. Every one of those is the bedrock of the *Tornadic Murderous God* we met at the outset. So, how can those be God? How can those be love? How can those be real power? How can those give meaning to the world? How can they give meaning to human existence? They can't. They don't. Those false and truthy idols don't deserve anyone's allegiance.

It is necessary to exile those deadly and truthy ideologies, since apart from changing and committing not to continue the past atrocities, the mere recognition of these catastrophes is worthless. That is why it was unavoidable to do the work of identifying some examples of divine truthiness that infect heads and hearts.

The Apostle Paul reassures us the infection will not do us in because the power of "Love is patient" (1 Cor 13:4). Love works as a genuine Tathata-Tau-Tao power *made perfect in weakness* that does not make love into a meaningless riddle. The rigid power of divine truthiness with its enforcer God who is easily bruised, easily offended, jealous, and infested with deceptions melts away in Paul's vision, because love "is not jealous . . . is not pompous . . . is not inflated . . . is not rude . . . does not seek its own interests . . . is not quick-tempered . . . does not brood over injury . . . does not rejoice over wrongdoing but rejoices with the truth" (1 Cor 13:4–6). Wholesome notions of power provide the courage needed to seek replacements for those desecrations of God. And the Apostle Paul provides hope that those abusive dogmas are not going to be the final word when he assures us that "love never fails. If there are prophecies, they will be brought to nothing; if tongues, they will cease; if knowledge, it will be brought to nothing. For we know partially and we prophesy partially, but when the perfect comes, the partial will pass away" (1 Cor 13:8). And that perfection is the *dynamic perfectioning* known as the God who is powerful love.

Our increased sensitivity to hurtful ideologies and idolatries might leave us feeling desperate: *if not even the things I clung to as absolutely true are true, then what's left?* The discovery of *Tathata-Tau-Tao* power—the kind of divine power that makes love flourish—is the solution. Actually, it turns out power cannot be separated from love. Whenever power and love are viciously separated, be alert for the risk of saying horrendous things about love—and even turning love into hate.

Tathata-Tau-Tao power reveals how persuasion, empathy, mutuality, and reciprocity combine as the principle factors in understanding authentic love. Since *God is love,* persuasion, empathy, mutuality, and reciprocity are therefore the principle factors in understanding who God is. And that means persuasion, empathy, mutuality, and reciprocity are the factors that determine what it means to be fully human, fully created in the divine image.

The wrong sort of power makes love a demonic riddle. But, Tathata-Tau-Tao power lets love reign harmoniously in head and heart alike. Tathata-Tau-Tao power liberates the symbol of love in a way that makes sense in both human and divine terms. The attempt I am undertaking here is to match what we know about the real sort of love in human terms with our language about divine love. Because of our perspective of continuity from divinity to the world—or our ability to say the universe is the sacrament of God—there is some hope that the evidence of this creation can give us some clue about its source, the divine love known as Omnicaritas.

The real love the Apostle Paul describes in 1 Corinthians 13 is made possible not by the gross indecencies and tragedies of divine truthiness. Rather, the real love described by Paul is made intelligible and real by these: persuasive power, which is the power perfected by weakness known to us in Tathata-Tau-Tao; empathy, which blossoms as the mutuality of solitude and solidarity; and the reciprocity of gratitude and generosity. Every effort to remove divine truthiness is an effort to encounter a love that is really love! When God is love, Omnicaritas is the real meaning of the genuine Tathata-Tau-Tao power of love.

Chapter 24

Divinity Is Powerful Love

In this journey, we have ventured into problems in our understandings of God, calling the whole catalogue of problematic approaches to understating God a *regime of divine truthiness*. Then, we dealt with the center of gravity for that violent and oppressive regime: highly problematic notions of power that do not work with the basic biblical intuition that *God is love*. In order to free ourselves from the shackles of doctrines of corrosive power, we set about discovering in the hearts of three world religions a wonderful alternative, a wonderful sort of *gentle and efficacious power of mutual becoming, power perfected in weakness, where the submissive overcomes the strong that everyone knows is true*—which fits better with the imperative to recognize that *God really is love*. Our investigations into Tathata, Tau, and Tao have allowed us to move beyond mere complaints against divine truthiness, build upon the discoveries about genuine power, and enter into a more beautiful realm where we come to a bright and meaningful understanding of powerful love. When the regime of divine truthiness is swept away, we are at last no longer beset by bizarre and incoherent notions of power that have too long made love into a perplexing riddle.

In light of Tathata-Tau-Tao power, we can now understand the power of all-love—Omnicaritas—is the real meaning of omnipotence. It is precisely the powerful all-lovingness of divinity—Omnicaritas—that is the most inclusively perfect category for divinity, the most exhaustive category for divinity, and the most definitive category for divinity. If we judge all the other notions of God through the lens of divine Omnicaritas, we will at once better understand the secondary characteristics, and also thereby wipe away falsified notions of power; wipe away falsified notions of divinity. The proper understanding of divine Omnicaritas will, like a gentle and steady flame, melt away the calcified accretions of divine truthiness we have applied to God. Or better yet, our profound understanding of divine

Omnicaritas will act like the flowing river, absorbing away the jagged edges of the of our broken, misleading, and dangerous ideas about divine love and divine power.

By now we have been sufficiently awakened to the insidious heart-and-mind worms of divine truthiness that we will be brim full with eagerness to set aside our certainty, and dare fearlessly to enter into realms of unknowing and doubt. The promise of reward is great: genuine Tathata-Tau-Tao power teaches a true understanding of love.

And *love is another word for the power to be of all things*, since as Julian says, "everything has being through the love of God."[1] Omnicaritas is the originating source and the power of being for the universe, which means the universe is the supreme sacrament, the visible aspect of the invisible divinity.

So, we are at last equipped with notions of power that are coherent with a genuine love theology of Omnicaritas. We proceed, assured of a God who creates a world that reflects its creator, a God of honest truth who deals with us lovingly.

It turns out God *is* love—but only when:

- love works by the interdependent origination power of mutual becoming (Tathata);

- love is peaceable, gentle, compliant, and merciful power perfected in weakness (Tau);

- love is watercourse power with submissiveness so strong it melts mountains (Tao).

Think of a world filled with people striving to imitate powerful love like that. Think of a world where affection and strength are joined.[2] Think of a world where we have ended divine truthiness, once and for all.

---

1. Julian of Norwich, *Showings*, 183.
2. Pope Francis, *Laudato Si'*, 53.

Chapter 25

The End of Divine Truthiness

We are created in the image and likeness of the powerful Omnicaritas that loves a universe of mutual becoming into existence. And it is at this point where we can at last banish the Tornadic and Murderous God. The violent and enforced regime of divine truthiness creates ruptures in the heart and mind of humanity, creates ruptures in the interrelationship between the world and God. We have been seeking wholeness as persons of head and heart, which means to be persons of holistic spirit and body. We have declared that it is thoroughly inhumane when divine truthiness uproots hearts from minds and banishes intellect from feeling.

This journey has led us to notions of divine love and notions of divine power that do not contradict one another. This journey has made it possible for us to immerse ourselves in an interrelated vision of universe and divinity. We have escaped the divine truthiness that seeks to "protect" God from the world of mutual becoming. What weak and fragile God is it that requires our feeble protections, anyway? Instead of that crumbling and embarrassing deity whose power is the rigid force of the coercive bully, we have come to know a God who is really love with the genuine power of Omnicaritas. We have come to know a God who creates by the gentle Tathata-Tau-Tao power of love; watercourse Tao power of submissive weakness that overcomes the strong; self-emptying Tau power perfected in weakness; the Tathata power of mutual becoming.

And on this journey we have rescued ourselves from dangerous ideas of divine truthiness that imply something inherently evil or wrong with the world of change, the world of mutual becoming. Far from being inherently evil or inherently wrong, we are now in a position to recognize in every single creature the sublime inheritance of divine love. And we can begin to see humanity as a continuous elaboration of the power of divine love. In fact we can see in every creature a continuation of the divine love: non-contentious power perfected in weakness unfolding in brilliant mutuality of becoming.

With new minds and new hearts, freed from the shackles of divine truthiness, we are no longer forced to believe the absurdity that hate is love. Instead, we can now diagnose absurdity as absurdity. We have seen that Martin Luther King, Jr. was right when he said, "power without love is reckless and abusive, and . . . love without power is sentimental and anemic."[1] Now that we can understand and feel the harmonious Tathata-Tau-Tao power of empathetic love, we banish the false power that destroys love. Our proper inheritance is our ability to be who we are created to be: people urged toward greater depths and heights of love. We might live in the untidy middle, in-MUNU. But right here in-MUNU we embody the further elaboration of great promise, and the ongoing life of the divine loving power, Omnicaritas, pressing toward ever-richer fulfillment.

Hearts and minds overflowing with the inexpressible delight of love[2] herald the *End of Divine Truthiness*. Now that divine Tathata-Tau-Tao power and divine empathetic love called Omnicaritas sustain and support one another, we can finally proclaim, without reservation, without asterisk:

Love is the power of God.
God is love. Powerful, powerful love.
And that's the WORD.
Amen.

---

1. King, ""Where Do We Go from Here?"
2. Benedict, *RB 1980*, prologue, 49.

Afterword: A Personal Note

No one has ever seen God. Yet, if we love one another,
God remains in us and his love is brought to perfection in us.

1 JOHN 4:12

I have alluded to my own personal experiences in just a few scant places in this book. I know it is not mainly about me. But I cannot ignore the roots of my own personal quest to find the power that is compatible with genuine love. In a way, this entire project is about making sense of the world and God, for myself—*though I hope it helps you too!*

I grew up in a home with two very different parents: a mother gifted with a passion for empathetic love, but who at the time often did not have the power to make it potent; and a father who was at war with his family of origin, and who ruled our nuclear family with violence, coercion, and intimidation. All the while, we would go to church—parading in late to the front-and-center pew so everyone could see us. Mortifying. And every Sunday my parents, and I, and my kid sister, and kid brother listened to talk of the truthy God who ruled the world as his possession through an omnipotent will and an absolute morality. The God we met at Saint John's was also literally male. That was made clear to me when a liberal cantor changed a hymn to use more inclusive God-language, in response to which my dad raged for a week. We never sang *that* again. Every day my dad imitated the God we met in church. The God we met in church demanded my mom and sister *know their place* (thank God *that* didn't stick). The supreme owner of our house was a little truthy god zealously imitating the divine punisher, the divine bully. Our resident truthy idol enforced his will through the power of his stuporous alcoholic rage.

An example: I remember being a seventh-grader, struggling with math. One Saturday night of homework turned into a nightmare when my dad asked if he could help. The more I failed, the angrier he got. The angrier he got, the less clearly I could think. At last he threw me to the ground, picked me up, and pushed me against the wall so I would have nowhere to go when he whipped me with his belt for being bad at math. Then he sent me to my room to try again. My whole body tensed with terror and frustration and the pencil snapped in my hand. When I was summoned back to report my next failure, he saw the broken pencil and knew that if *he* were to break a pencil it would be out of defiance and spite, so he slammed me against the wall and punched me in the nose so I would bleed for those imaginary offenses. Of course I left and failed again. Repeat. I begged to stop, but this went on past midnight, when he finally passed out. My mom came to my room to tend my bloody nose, and told me he did this because he loved me.

The next morning we went to church to hear stories about the Father God's beloved Son, who realized he had to die and begged to stop it. But the abusive Father God refused the plea. The divine plan required the suffering and death of the Son. There it is. My dad was living his theology. My dad had been fed a steady diet of garbage about an all-powerful Father God whose will is the torture, abuse, and execution of his beloved Son. And it was all for our own good. It was all for love. My mom was fed the same diet (we all were). So, it is no wonder she could utter the words that also imitated the truthy theology: *sure he beats you up—but it is all done out of love.*

If God is the Absolute Torturing Father whose love is violence, then no one in my life exemplified the image of that God more than my dad. What further permission beyond the divine blessing and command can a violent person hope for?

I know that my little life is only a sliver of a microcosm of the bigger problem. I can't watch the news without seeing people living out wrong and deadly theologies—imitating a God whose love is hate, and bringing devastation and terror to our world. Terrifying theologies prop up people enchanted by authoritarianism, despotism, violence, and oppression. If God gives aid and comfort to oppressive, violent, authoritarian despots, then I want nothing to do with it. If that has to be God, then I'd have to agree with the atheists.

So, I have staked my work as a theologian on the hope that there is another kind of power, another kind of powerful love that is the truth of

God. My search has brought me to denounce the false and truthy God. My search has brought me to the heart of the Buddha, whose awakening taught him that real power flourishes in reality as interdependent co-arising or mutual becoming. My search has brought me to the heart of the Tao, which revealed that real power overcomes rigid enforcement with the power of non-contention—the waterpower to absorb stone away, and move mountains. My search has brought me into the heart of Jesus, whose life, teaching, death, and resurrection all reveal that real power is peaceable, gentle, compliant, and merciful, and is made perfect in weakness. My search has cleared my mind and heart from the specters of the deadly, fake, and truthy God whose love is violent hate. My search convinces me that the truest thing that can be said is this:

> God is powerful love
> —but, more to the point—
> powerful love is God.

Paul Joseph Greene
January 19, 2017

Glossary

MuNu: *Alpha* (A) and *Omega* (Ω) is a way of symbolically saying God is the beginning and the end of all things by invoking the first and last letters of the Greek alphabet. Sure, divine love resides at the beginning and the end, but we do not reside at the Alpha or the Omega. We are somewhere in the middle. I propose that love is not only Alpha and Omega, but also what we could call MuNu—the muddled middle. MuNu is the combination of the *middle two letters* of the Greek alphabet. MuNu is a symbol for the middle of reality as we encounter it. MuNu implies impermanence of transformation from the Mu to the Nu. MuNu also implies continuity, for in order for the arising of Nu, first Mu must arise. MuNu implies a real relationship with the beginning, the Alpha, and a real relationship with the end, the Omega. MuNu implies a continuity of interdependence from the Alpha to the MuNu, through to the Omega.

Omnicaritas: This is the best category to describe God since it means the All-Love, or all-loving. Omnicaritas is the true meaning of omnipotence because the divine power is the divine love.

Perfectioning: In place of perfection it is better to speak of "dynamic perfectioning." Turning the word *perfection* into a gerund highlights that static perfection is an illusion. If anything resembles *perfection*, it must be a process whereby the richness of dynamic love is best understood as *growth*, *maturation*, and *increase*, instead of static immutability. Perfectioning is a gentle reminder that genuine perfection is not some static lump. Rather, perfection is dynamic perfectioning, always on the move and on the way.

Pratitya Samutpada: The Buddha's awakened insight that all phenomena arise interdependently: the interdependent co-arising of all phenomena. Here it is referred to as *mutual becoming*, the Tathata of reality.

Tao: The Way in philosophical Taoism. Here it symbolizes the genuine power of reality, where the weak overcomes the strong, and the soft overcomes the rigid—a truth known by all, yet difficult to implement. Tao is the Taoist symbol of non-contentious water power that does without doing, and prevails without enforcement.

Tathata: A Buddhist term for *how things really are*. Tathata is often translated as "suchness," or the as-it-is-ness of things. We can only ever approximate Tathata in our concepts and ideas because of the deeply perspectival and symbolic nature of our language and existence. The Tathata of our universe is the interdependent co-arising of all phenomena. Tathata is something like *the bare existence of all things* (Dionysius the Areopagite). Tathata is something like *the inner nature* of things (Taoist *hsian sheng*). Tathata is the Buddhist symbol of power as mutual becoming.

Tau: This is just the anglicized transliteration of the letter T (uppercase) or τ (lowercase) in the Greek alphabet, and really it is just the letter that approximates the shape of the cross of Christ. I came across this word, Tau, in my reading of Saint Bonaventure's *Life of St. Francis*. To be marked with a Tau is to live a life contrary to the powers of the world. It is to live a life of generous relinquishment, rather than a life of greedy acquisition. It is to live a life of grateful reception, rather than entitlement. It is to live a life of conformity to the example of Christ, the example of the cross of Christ. To be marked with the Tau is to be marked with total generosity and total gratitude. Tau is the Christian symbol of peaceable, gentle, compliant, and merciful power perfected in weakness.

Truthiness: One-sided junk thought. Truthiness can mean either over-relying on intellect to the detriment of feeling, or over-relying on feeling to the detriment of intellect in trying to understand something. Truthiness is a dehumanizing, one-sided approach to knowing or feeling. The division is what diminishes and dehumanizes us. Truthiness also means believing what one prefers to be true even when the facts contradict that belief. *Divine truthiness* is junk thought about God or religion, where errors in theology lead to non-sensical notions like love defined as hatred. Another way to indicate *divine truthiness* is to refer to the *truthy God*, the God who is an idol of our false construction, especially when power and love ruin each other.

Bibliography

Abe, Masao. "Kenotic God and Dynamic Sunyata." In *The Emptying God: A Buddhist-Jewish-Christian Conversation*, edited by John B. Cobb, Christopher Ives, and Masao Abe, 3–65. Faith Meets Faith. Maryknoll, NY: Orbis, 1990.

Anselm of Canterbury. *Basic Writings: Proslogium; Monologium; Gaunilon's on Behalf of the Fool; Cur Deus Homo*. Edited by Sidney Norton. 17th printing. La Salle, IL: Open Court, 1993.

Aronson, Martin. *Jesus and Lao Tzu: The Parallel Sayings*. 1st ed. Berkeley, CA: Seastone, 2000.

Benedict of Nursia. *RB 1980: The Rule of St. Benedict in Latin and English with Notes*. Edited by Timothy Fry. Collegeville, MN: Liturgical, 1981.

Blumenfeld, Warren J. "Tragic Shootings Blamed on Denying Prayer in Schools and Public Square." *Huffington Post*, December 20, 2012. http://www.huffingtonpost.com/warren-j-blumenfeld/tragic-shootings-blamed-on-denying-prayer-in-schools-and-public-square_b_2319700.html.

Boff, Leonardo. *Cry of the Earth, Cry of the Poor*. Ecology and Justice. Maryknoll, NY: Orbis, 1997.

———. *Global Civilization: Challenges to Society and to Christianity*. Cross Cultural Theologies. Oakville, CT: Equinox, 2005.

Bonaventure. *Bonaventure*. Edited by Ewert H. Cousins. Classics of Western Spirituality. New York: Paulist, 1978.

Brierly, Michael W. "Naming a Quiet Revolution: The Panentheistic Turn in Modern Theology." In *Whom We Live and Move and Have Our Being: Panentheistic Reflections on God's Presence in a Scientific World*, edited by Philip Clayton and A. R. Peacocke, 1–15. Grand Rapids, MI: W.B. Eerdmans, 2004.

Brown, Peter Robert Lamont. *The Body and Society: Men, Women, and Sexual Renunciation in Early Christianity*. Lectures on the History of Religions, new series, no. 13. New York: Columbia University Press, 1988.

Catechism of the Catholic Church. 2nd ed. http://ccc.usccb.org/flipbooks/catechism/index.html#88

Cobb, John B., and David Ray Griffin. *Process Theology: An Introductory Exposition*. Philadelphia: Westminster, 1976.

Colbert, Stephen T., host. *The Colbert Report*. Season 1, episode 1. Comedy Central, October 17, 2005. http://www.cc.com/episodes/jnv7om/the-colbert-report-october-17--2005---stone-phillips-season-1-ep-01001.

————. *The Colbert Report*. Season 2, episode 132. Comedy Central, October 17, 2006. http://www.cc.com/episodes/sm586a/the-colbert-report-october-17--2006---richard-dawkins-season-2-ep-02132.

————. *The Colbert Report*. Season 2, episode 148. Comedy Central, November 28, 2006. http://www.cc.com/episodes/sfxpvl/the-colbert-report-november-28--2006---harry-shearer-season-2-ep-02148

————. *The Colbert Report*. Season 2, episode 156. Comedy Central, December 12, 2006. http://www.cc.com/episodes/80io3s/the-colbert-report-december-12--2006---dan-savage-season-2-ep-02156.

————. *The Colbert Report*. Season 4, episode 53. Comedy Central, April 22, 2008. http://www.cc.com/episodes/wo4arm/the-colbert-report-april-22--2008---susan-jacoby-season-4-ep-04053.

————. *The Colbert Report*. Season 8, episode 19. Comedy Central, November 9, 2011. http://www.cc.com/episodes/xtcc3t/the-colbert-report-november-9--2011---james-martin-season-8-ep-08019.

————. *The Late Show with Stephen Colbert*. Season 1, episode 178. CBS, July 18, 2016. https://goo.gl/tPDQqD.

————. *The Late Show with Stephen Colbert*. Season 2, episode 157. CBS, June 9, 2017. https://goo.gl/TZYhF5.

Coleman, Monica A. *Making a Way out of No Way: A Womanist Theology*. Innovations: African American Religious Thought. Minneapolis: Fortress, 2008.

Cyprian of Carthage. *Treatise 10: On Jealousy and Envy*. Translated by Robert Ernest Wallis. In *Ante-Nicene Fathers*, vol. 5, edited by Alexander Roberts, James Donaldson, and A. Cleveland Coxe. Buffalo, NY: Christian Literature, 1886. http://www.newadvent.org/fathers/050710.htm.

Davies, Paul. "Teleology without Teleology: Purpose through Emergent Complexity." In *Whom We Live and Move and Have Our Being: Panentheistic Reflections on God's Presence in a Scientific World,* edited by Philip Clayton and A. R. Peacocke, 95–108. Grand Rapids, MI: W.B. Eerdmans, 2004.

Dickerson, John. "Face the Nation Transcript December 25, 2016: Colbert, CBS Correspondents Roundtable." http://www.cbsnews.com/news/face-the-nation-transcript-december-25-2016-colbert-correspondents-panel/.

Dionysius the Areopagite. *Dionysius, the Areopagite, on the Divine Names and Mystical Theology*. Edited by C. E. Rolt. Translations of Christian Literature 1: Greek Texts. New York: Macmillan, 1920.

Edwards, Denis. "A Relational and Evolving Universe Unfolding within the Dynamism of the Divine Communion." *In Whom We Live and Move and Have Our Being: Panentheistic Reflections on God's Presence in a Scientific World*, edited by Philip Clayton and A. R. Peacocke, 199–210. Grand Rapids, MI: W.B. Eerdmans, 2004.

Francis, Pope. *Laudato Si': On Care for Our Common Home*. Huntington, IN: Our Sunday Visitor Publishing Division, 2015.

Freire, Paulo. *Pedagogy of the Oppressed*. New York: Herder, 1970.

Friedman, Megan. "Here's the Full Transcript of Meryl Streep's Powerful Golden Globes Speech." *Harper's Bazaar*, January 8, 2017. http://www.harpersbazaar.com/culture/film-tv/news/a19828/meryl-street-golden-globes-speech-transcript/.

Gladstone, Brooke. "Troubador of Truthiness." December 22, 2006. http://www.onthemedia.org/2006/dec/22/troubadour-of-truthiness/transcript/.

Gomes, Peter J. *The Good Book: Reading the Bible with Mind and Heart*. New York: W. Morrow, 1996.

Griffin, David Ray. *Reenchantment without Supernaturalism: A Process Philosophy of Religion*. Cornell Studies in the Philosophy of Religion. Ithaca, NY: Cornell University Press, 2001.

Hanh, Thich Nhat. *No Death, No Fear: Comforting Wisdom for Life*. Berkeley, CA: Riverhead, 2002.

Harris, Sam. *The End of Faith: Religion, Terror, and the Future of Reason*. New York: Norton, 2005.

Hartshorne, Charles. *Omnipotence and Other Theological Mistakes*. Albany: State University of New York Press, 1984.

Hellwig, Monika K., "Eschatology." In *Systematic Theology*, edited by Francis Schüssler Fiorenza and John P. Galvin, 2:349–72. Minneapolis: Fortress, 1991.

Hewitt Suchocki, Marjorie. "In Search of Justice: Religious Pluralism from a Feminist Perspective." In *The Myth of Christian Uniqueness: Toward a Pluralistic Theology of Religions*, edited by John Hick and Paul F. Knitter, 149–61. Faith Meets Faith. Maryknoll, NY: Orbis, 1987.

Hoff, Benjamin. *The Tao of Pooh*. 1st ed. New York: E.P. Dutton, 1982.

———. *The Te of Piglet*. 1st ed. London: Egmont, 1992.

Irenaeus of Lyons. *The Scandal of the Incarnation: Irenaeus against the Heresies*. Translated by John Saward, edited by Hans Urs von Balthasar. San Francisco: Ignatius, 1990.

Johnson, Elizabeth A. *Quest for the Living God: Mapping Frontiers in the Theology of God*. New York: Continuum, 2007.

Jones, Serene. *Feminist Theory and Christian Theology: Cartographies of Grace*. Guides to Theological Inquiry. Minneapolis: Fortress, 2000.

Julian of Norwich. *Showings*. Edited by Edmund Colledge and James Walsh. Classics of Western Spirituality. New York: Paulist, 1978.

Kasper, Walter. *Jesus the Christ*. New York: Paulist, 1977.

Kaufman, Gordon D. "Religious Diversity, Historical Consciousness, and Christian Theology." In *The Myth of Christian Uniqueness: Toward a Pluralistic Theology of Religions*, edited by John Hick and Paul F. Knitter. Faith Meets Faith Series. Maryknoll, NY: Orbis, 1987.

King, Martin Luther, Jr. "Where Do We Go from Here?" Delivered at the 11th Annual SCLC Convention, Atlanta, Georgia, August 16, 1967. https://kinginstitute.stanford. edu/king-papers/documents/where-do-we-go-here-delivered-11th-annual-sclc-convention.

Kiriyama, Seiyu. *21st Century, the Age of Sophia: The Wisdom of Greek Philosophy and the Wisdom of the Buddha*. Translated by Rande Brown Ouchi. Tokyo: Hirakawa Shuppan, 2000.

Knitter, Paul F. *One Earth, Many Religions: Multifaith Dialogue and Global Responsibility*. Maryknoll, NY: Orbis, 1995.

———. *No Other Name?: A Critical Survey of Christian Attitudes toward the World Religions*. American Society of Missiology Series 7. Maryknoll, NY: Orbis, 1985.

———. *Without Buddha I Could Not Be a Christian*. Oxford: Oneworld, 2009.

Lao Tzu. *Tao Te Ching*. Translated by Dim Cheuk Lau. Penguin Classics. Baltimore: Penguin, 1963.

Leech, Kenneth. *Spirituality and Pastoral Care*. Cambridge, MA: Cowley, 1989.

Lerner, Alan Jay. *Camelot*. New York: Chappell, 1961.

Luther, Martin. *On Christian Liberty.* Translated by Harold J. Grimm and W. A. Lambert. Facets. Minneapolis: Fortress, 2003.

Macy, Joanna. *Mutual Causality in Buddhism and General Systems Theory: The Dharma of Natural Systems.* Albany, NY: State University of New York Press, 1991.

Matthews, Chris. *Hardball with Chris Matthews.* NBC News, May 21, 2013. Transcript at http://www.nbcnews.com/id/51968582/ns/msnbc-hardball_with_chris_matthews/t/hardball-chris-matthews-tuesday-may-st/#.WQJi7VMrKhY.

McDaniel, Jay B. *With Roots and Wings: Christianity in an Age of Ecology and Dialogue.* Ecology and Justice Series. Maryknoll, NY: Orbis, 1995.

Megathlin, Carol. "The God of the Tornado (Opinion from Carol Megathlin)." May 21, 2013. http://www.al.com/opinion/index.ssf/2013/05/the_god_of_the_tornado_opinion.html.

Moltmann, Jurgen. *The Crucified God: The Cross of Christ as the Foundation and Criticism of Christian Theology.* 1st US ed. New York: Harper & Row, 1974.

———. *God in Creation: A New Theology of Creation and the Spirit of God.* The Gifford Lectures 1984–1985. Minneapolis: Fortress, 1993.

———. "God Is Unselfish Love." In *The Emptying God: A Buddhist-Jewish-Christian Conversation,* edited by John B. Cobb, Christopher Ives, and Masao Abe, 116–24. Faith Meets Faith. Maryknoll, NY: Orbis, 1990.

———. *The Trinity and the Kingdom: The Doctrine of God.* Minneapolis: Fortress, 1993.

Newbigin, Lesslie. *Foolishness to the Greeks: The Gospel and Western Culture.* Grand Rapids: Eerdmans, 1986.

Obama, Barack H. "President Obama State of the Union Address 2016 Full Transcript Text." *Christian Post,* Politics, January 12, 2016. http://www.christianpost.com/news/president-obama-state-of-the-union-address-2016-full-transcript-text-154775/page3.html.

Panikkar, Raimundo. *Christophany: The Fullness of Man.* Faith Meets Faith. Maryknoll, NY: Orbis, 2004.

———. *The Intrareligious Dialogue.* New York: Paulist, 1978.

Pieris, Aloysius. *Love Meets Wisdom: A Christian Experience of Buddhism.* Faith Meets Faith. Maryknoll, NY: Orbis, 1988.

"'Post-Truth' Declared Word of the Year by Oxford Dictionaries." BBC News, UK edition, November 16, 2016. http://www.bbc.com/news/uk-37995600.

"President Obama's Speech at Prayer Vigil for Newtown Shooting Victims (Full Transcript)." *Washington Post,* Politics, December 16, 2012. https://www.washingtonpost.com/politics/president-obamas-speech-at-prayer-vigil-for-newtown-shooting-victims-full-transcript/2012/12/16/f764bf8a-47dd-11e2-ad54-580638ede391_story.html?utm_term=.55ca88733c14.

Ruether, Rosemary Radford. "Feminism and Jewish-Christian Dialogue." In *The Myth of Christian Uniqueness: Toward a Pluralistic Theology of Religions,* edited by John Hick and Paul F. Knitter, 137–48. Faith Meets Faith. Maryknoll, NY: Orbis, 1987.

Segundo, Juan Luis. *An Evolutionary Approach to Jesus of Nazareth.* Translated and edited by John Drury. Jesus of Nazareth Yesterday and Today 5. Maryknoll, NY: Orbis, 1988.

Simonaitis, Susan M. "Teaching as Conversation." In *The Scope of Our Art : The Vocation of the Theological Teacher,* edited by L. Gregory Jones and Stephanie Paulsell, 99–119. Grand Rapids: Eerdmans, 2002.

Sivaraska, Sulak. *The Wisdom of Sustainability: Buddhist Economics for the 21st Century.* Kihei, Hawai'i: Koa, 2009.

Smart, Ninian, and Steven Konstantine. *Christian Systematic Theology in a World Context.* World Christian Theology Series. Minneapolis: Fortress, 1991.

Spong, John Shelby. *Rescuing the Bible from Fundamentalism: A Bishop Rethinks the Meaning of Scripture.* San Francisco: HarperCollins, 1991.

———. *Why Christianity Must Change or Die: A Bishop Speaks to Believers in Exile.* San Francisco: HarperCollins, 1998.

Sponheim, Paul R. *Love's Availing Power: Imaging God, Imagining the World.* Minneapolis: Fortress, 2011.

Suchocki, Marjorie. *God-Christ-Church: A Practical Guide to Process Theology.* New York: Crossroad, 1982.

Teilhard de Chardin, Pierre. *Christianity and Evolution.* London: Collins, 1971.

———. *The Divine Milieu.* Translated by Siôn Cowell. Portland: Sussex Academic, 2004.

Thomas Aquinas, and Peter Kreeft. *A Summa of the Summa: The Essential Philosophical Passages of St. Thomas Aquinas' Summa Theologica.* San Francisco: Ignatius, 1990.

Tillich, Paul. *Biblical Religion and the Search for Ultimate Reality.* Richard Lectures, University of Virginia. Chicago: University of Chicago Press, 1955.

———. *Christianity and the Encounter of the World Religions.* Bampton Lectures in America 14. New York: Columbia University Press, 1963.

———. *The New Being.* New York: Scribner, 1955.

———. *Systematic Theology.* 3 vols. Chicago: University of Chicago Press, 1951.

Ward, Keith. "The World as the Body of God: A Panentheistic Metaphor." In *Whom We Live and Move and Have Our Being: Panentheistic Reflections on God's Presence in a Scientific World,* edited by Philip Clayton and A. R. Peacocke, 62–72. Grand Rapids, MI: W.B. Eerdmans, 2004.

Watts, Alan, and Al Chung-liang Huang. *Tao: The Watercourse Way.* 1st ed. New York: Pantheon, 1975.

Whitehead, Alfred North. *Adventures of Ideas.* New York: Macmillan, 1933.

———. *Modes of Thought.* New York: Macmillan, 1938.

Whitehead, Alfred North, David Ray Griffin, and Donald W. Sherburne. *Process and Reality: An Essay in Cosmology.* Gifford Lectures 1927–1928. Corrected ed. New York: Free Press, 1929.

Whitman, Walt. *Leaves of Grass.* 1st Vintage Books/Library of America ed. New York: Vintage Books/Library of America, 1992.

Names Index

Subject Index

power perfected in weakness, 129–33,
135–37, 140, 144–45, 165,
171–74, 180
pratitya samutpada, 20, 22, 109–110,
163, 179

quantum entanglement, 23, 25

radical egalitarianism, 134
reception (receptivity), 18, 30, 32, 35–
37, 68, 84–86, 88, 118, 180
reciprocity (reciprocal), x, 27, 35–37, 39,
47–48, 61, 63, 76, 83–85, 88, 95,
112, 118, 169
rigid power, 12, 87, 96, 101, 107, 109,
146, 151–53, 168, 173, 176, 180
ripple effect, 25
Rule of St. Benedict, 39, 113–15, 174n2

Sandy Hook Elementary, 4–5
self-emptying (see kenosis), 125–27,
129–30, 144, 162–64, 173
solidarity, x 21–22, 26, 33–34, 37, 47, 58,
62, 95, 109, 111, 163–64, 169
solitude, x, 33–34, 37, 58, 62, 111, 169
Son of God, 37, 121, 126, 128, 131, 134,
136–38
sow-reaping, 23
static perfection, 60, 68–72, 179
status quo, 50, 55, 61, 65–67, 95, 133
submission, 158–59, 164–65, 171–73
suffering (divine suffering, and divine
inflicted suffering), ix, 3, 32, 36,
59–62, 68, 85, 95, 112, 119, 121,
126, 128, 138–45, 164, 168, 176
suffering (victim), xvi, 31–32, 36,-37,
41, 50. 60–61, 73–75, 80, 84–85,
95, 138–39, 141–44, 168, 176
Supreme Owner God, 77–80, 89, 103,
122, 128, 167

tai chi, 153
Tao, 13n8, 107, 146, 147, 148n2, 148–
53, 153n20, 155–65, 171–73,
177, 180
Tao te Ching, 71, 104, 146, 148–52, 155,
157–59, 162–63

Taoism (Taoist), x, xvi, xviii, 13, 13n8,
22, 29, 29n3, 104, 106–7, 145–
47, 147n1, 148, 150–56, 158–59,
161–63, 180
Tathata, 17–21, 25–26, 28, 30, 32, 46,
48, 54, 68n1, 71, 73–74, 87, 104,
107, 109–117, 128, 132, 145–46,
148–49, 152, 157–58, 160,
162–64, 171–73
Tathata-Tau-Tao, 107, 158, 165, 168–69,
171–74
Tau, 107, 117–25, 127–30, 132, 134–36,
138–46, 150–53, 158–59, 164–
65, 171, 173, 180
temptations, 92, 130–32, 138, 144, 168
terrorism (terror, terrorist), vi, xviii,
xviiin6, 5–6, 32, 48, 62, 73, 102,
176
Ten Commandments, 64
theism (theist, monotheism), 13, 40–41,
53, 54n4, 58, 83
theodicy, 59n2
theological anthropology, 43–52, 55, 57,
77–79, 98n6, 122
theology, xvii-xviii, 5, 12, 23, 29n3, 30,
43–52, 55, 57, 59–61, 64, 66, 68,
77, 82, 85, 87n17, 91, 100–101,
103–4, 111, 114, 116, 123, 125,
127, 133, 135, 139, 146, 172,
176, 180
Tornadic God, 3–4, 6, 168, 173
Trinity, 3, 22, 47–48
trophic cascade, 24–25
truthiness, x, xvi-xviii, 1, 6–13, 19–20,
29–30, 35, 37, 39, 41, 44, 51–53,
55–58, 61–68, 68n1, 71–72, 74,
76–77, 79, 84, 89–94, 100, 102–
4, 106–7, 109, 111–13, 116–17,
119–25, 127–28, 130–31, 133,
137–40, 144–48, 150, 152–53,
154n25, 155–56, 158–60, 164,
167, 168–69, 171–74, 180
truthy, xvii, 9, 9n12, 13, 31–32, 36–37,
39–41, 43–44, 50, 52–53, 56, 58,
60–61, 64–67, 77–81, 83–85,
90, 92–94, 99, 101, 103–4, 106,
116–17, 120–21, 123, 125, 128,

Scripture Index

Old Testament

New Testament